from the

kitchens of

MaryAnn

This book
is for you!

Best

Meditz

2015

NOT FOR YOU
Family Narratives of Denial & Comfort Foods

Book One

Nandita Godbole
2017

TURMERIC PRESS

All photographs are © Nandita Godbole, 2017
Food Styling & Graphic Design: Nandita Godbole
Editor & EBook Conversion: R. Umashankar

Publisher's Cataloging-in-Publication Data
Godbole, Nandita
Not For You: Family Narratives of Denial & Comfort Foods: Book One / Nandita Godbole
ISBN: 978-1-940957-14-2

1. History 2. Indian. 3. Cooking.
Fiction
Limited Release, First Edition

ABOUT THE COVER

Red: Kumkum, vermillion, life, strength, blood, sacred, awakening, the color of 'Devi' or 'Shakti.'

Yellow: Turmeric, holy, healing, sanctification, purification, centering, calming.

White: Sandalwood, peace, the color of 'Vishnu,' the creator.

These colours paint many aspects of Hindu life, marking life events by their presence or absence, signifying movement from one phase of life to another, from innocence to worldliness to spiritual fulfillment and transcendence. And of the three, kumkum and turmeric are most prevalent in a Hindu life. When kumkum and turmeric come together, they represent the balance between and the merging of the every day, the mundane and the ordinary, with the divine, the holy and the omnipresent energy. For some, these two together represent the essence of life. In an uncanny coincidence, two important pieces of an Indian kitchen are cayenne pepper and turmeric, one red as the color of kumkum, the other, turmeric itself.

To a Hindu woman, these two, kumkum and turmeric represent coveted marks of identity, status, and of belonging to a sisterhood of married women. But these colors also tether her to social norms and domestic responsibilities, most often to the kitchen. When she dances between these two worlds: one communal, one personal, she creates a third space, a home, a place of comfort. While these two colours unite all life in the Indian subcontinent, they also represent unchallenged frontiers that define the identity of the Hindu woman.

Does this definition of womanhood change over time?

PREFACE

Is it a fictional story or are the people real?
To believe that this book is merely a story would be inaccurate. It is an unusual saga of twelve
main characters spanning more than 150 years. These characters emerged from encounters with
individuals like them. It makes the characters in this book partially real, but only barely. Who
would you like to meet: the apparition, their spirit, or their soul?

Is it a cookbook or a novel?
All foods have stories. This book includes longer stories about special foods, so this is a food-novel.

Is this book about religion?
No. Although religion plays a part for some of its characters, this narrative does not promote
any religious belief. Instead, some of the characters have very conflicting relationships with their
spirituality and its cultural baggage. Discover the flaws and the merits of their choices.

This book is about three complicated things: people, food, and life.

It is about men and women whose lives were ordinary by all conventional standards. Their lives
overlap in time, their decisions affect others, influence their foods, and their children experience the
cumulative actions of their elders.

It is one story and yet there are many stories within.

It is a story of persevering through tough times, personal struggles, and public crusades, about
prejudice and its aftermath.

It is a tale about humans being terribly flawed.

And what happens after the dust settles.

Nandita Godbole

2017

For Papa.
You endured so much with a smile.
This is our lesson.

CHAPTER ONE

The Puppeteer's Stories

1899, LUNAWA, RAJASTHAN

The mutiny of 1857 had flung its burning embers all over India. Even decades after it had erupted and had seemingly been resolved and perhaps the country had recovered from the brunt of the unrest, some villages in the receding shadows of their princely protection continued to smoulder, ever so slowly. Riots continued to erupt, some were bloodier than others. But when the strife blurred the lines between community, religion and the Company, it left horrific scars on all caught in its crossfire.

The desert state of Rajasthan was no different. Many kingdoms within its proud borders had suffered. Several smaller kingdoms chose to become princely states while others were absorbed into the British Raj. The new Rajputana Railways opened up the region in 1876 bringing new people to the princely state of Sirohi, and with it, unexpected changes.

Sheltered by the generosity of the royal families of both Sirohi and Udaipur, the village of Lunawa had remained protected. This small God-fearing wada (walled village) had enjoyed the privilege of participating in the many festivities and celebrations of both kingdoms. If the Maharana of Udaipur was not hosting a celebration to honour his wives or his daughter, the Rao of Sirohi was making plans to honour a deity, a travelling holy man, or a scholar. If the people of Lunawa were not heading to one fair eastwards towards Udaipur, they were planning for a communal visit to the Durga temples of Mt. Abu or the Dilwara temples to the west. It was a trouble-free community of humble people.

This went on for many years, until everything changed one day, in 1899. That March day started like every other; the festival of Holi was around the corner and the women were eager to begin preparations for the annual Gangaur celebrations. This festival seemingly humanised two Gods in the form of two dolls—Shiva became the male doll Gana, while his wife and consort, Gauri or Parvati became the second doll, Gaur (Gauri)—and celebrated their love and devotion as their own.

Women were planning their feasts and fasts and were setting aside time to darn their ghaghras (long skirts) and embellishing their oodhniys (head-scarves), hoping that their penance and prayers during the celebration would bestow long marriages and faithful spouses upon them. Childlike wonder and faith emerged in every woman for this festival.

But something was amiss that morning, the birds were quieter than usual. A little after the cool dew had evaporated and the men had headed out to the bajra fields, loud screams pierced through the walls of the wada. A few women returning from the village well stopped in their tracks to see a young boy with a slightly bloodied head running towards them, away from the fields; his feet kicking up sand and dust behind him. He was screaming.

"The thieves are here, Moti-ba, thieves!"

His young voice crackled and ripped through his throat. Today was different. Moti-ba heard the commotion and signalled her fourteen-year-old granddaughter, Johari, to set down her chores and go indoors. She was to check if the embers in their little mud-baked stove had cooled into ashes for scrubbing their breakfast utensils.

Their little hut was a safe place, sheltered within the wada. The single room served as a place to sleep or cook, the stoop was where anyone visiting sat. The walls of the hut were made of mud and straw; it kept them cool in the summer and kept out the winds at night. It was a simple hut for simple people.

They had made a buttery cha that morning with fresh milk from their water buffalos and warmed up last night's rotlas on the tavdi (shallow fry pan) for breakfast that morning. Johari's tohlu (shallow bowl) was smaller than Moti-ba's but held many things; her breakfast, lunch or dinner. Their meals were rustic, simple, essential, and served in kansa (bell metal) utensils that shone like liquid gold when scrubbed clean with the ashes from the stove. Johari would have to wait a little; the ashes were still warm.

Moti-ba was certain the little howling devil had decided to play another prank on the unsuspecting women in the wada, when it was only the travelling kawadia bhat (wandering storyteller), making his stop. These were Johari's favourite visitors. The gypsy-like kawadia bhats came through their village often carrying with them small magical boxes called kawads. Each kawadia bhat was different and their stories as unique as their kawads, that unfolded stories of Krishna's youth, or from the epics of the Ramayana or Mahabharat, or the relatively modern tales of the poet-saint Meera-bai, who was once a local princess. Some bhats brought puppets, others brought musical instruments. The entire village would gather to hear the kawadia bhats tell their stories well into the night. Moti-ba decided she was going to set this prankster straight once and for all. Grabbing her old knotted stick from the doorway, she walked on, muttering to herself.

"Wretched boy! Today he shall see, who the real thief is!"

The stick came from a tamarind tree from her own parents' home beyond Sirohi. It was as reliable as it was respected and feared by the villagers. Johari snickered under her breath knowing the poor boy was in trouble. She hoped that today's kawadia bhat had brought a kawad to tell the story of Meera-bai's life, her favourite princess saint, and sing some beautiful poetry about her devotion to her soul-mate, Lord Krishna.

Everyone in the village respectfully addressed Johari's grandmother as Moti-ba or elder mother. She was the village matron, the oldest in the village. Once known as Jona-ba, she was a stunningly tall beauty with dark eyes and a dark complexion to match. In her youth, her hair was long and always hidden beneath colourful oodhniys. Beautiful jewellery hung from her ears and neck, her wrists were often decked with colourful glass bangles and her palms were soft and mottled from the frequent applications of henna. One year she had caught the eye of a young farmer, Dhuni, at a wedding fair. Dhuni was smitten with her—they were married at the next wedding fair in the following year.

Communal wedding fairs were a common occurrence; several villages agreed upon an auspicious date, found a host village with a suitably sized temple and invited eligible young men and women from nearby with their families. It was a place for families to unite over matrimony and attracted holy men and palm readers, merchants of all types selling curios and trinkets to eager buyers, and curious women and portly old men who enjoyed people watching, cartwheels and rides. It was a convenient event, though sometimes chaotic, that attracted many ineligible young men and maidens hoping to catch the eye of their future spouses.

Jona-ba's fierce temperament was an attractive trait to Dhuni, as she ruled his heart and household with finesse and charm. She had spent many years watching her sisters and learned how to make her own words count. Dhuni realised he wanted to give Jona-ba more, and so, in exchange for a steady income, he went to serve in the Company as a sepoy. He entrusted his 2-acre bajra field in the care of the village elders, hoping they would watch over it and his young family in his absence. He would claim it all back when he returned. As he walked away from Lunawa to join the company, Jona-ba held their first born, Natthu on her hips, in her heart believing that Dhuni would return before long.

With Dhuni gone, the colours from Jona-ba's life slowly but surely began to drain. For some time the village elders watched over her and Natthu, occasionally bring her a portion of the harvest and sometimes help her with chores. She would get word that Dhuni was traveling across Rajasthan. But one afternoon, a few years after Dhuni had first left, word came that that the young man was caught in the crossfire of the unrest at Ulwur, a region just to the north and east of Jaipur, where the Narukas were struggling for territories. He was never returning home—the year was 1872.

Jona-ba now had to survive for her son, Natthu, without Dhuni. She quickly learned that she was now a destitute. The Company could not pay her Dhuni's back-wages and the elders would not return her fields yet because Natthu was far too young to take over. Perhaps the other widows and grandmothers in Lunawa might help, she hoped.

Jona-ba was a young widow, too proud to remarry, too headstrong to be desirable, and far too poor to be a good 'catch'. She was often left behind to watch over the homes when other women went to visit the fairs in the nearby villages, attend the Gangaur Festival or to visit Udaipur, Pali or Dilwara with their families. Being a widow also meant Jona-ba had to sit out weddings, birth and death rituals in her community because—those were the rules. She hoped for better days when Natthu was older. Time passed slowly and as a farmer yearned for rain, Jona-ba yearned for friendship and companionship in this village of happy families.

Natthu had no one to speak for him to bring him a suitable alliance. When he was old enough, a young girl's father from a nearby village came to visit Jona-ba. He was looking for a suitable spouse for his second daughter Sila. He had heard about Dhuni's sacrifice and proclaimed that the son of such a noble individual, Natthu, would be a suitable match for Sila. Secretly he was hoping to marry off his daughter without spending a lot of money. As a widow of limited means, Jona-ba would not want to host an elaborate wedding either as she could not attend it. Marrying his Sila to Natthu at a wedding fair would be a good compromise. He would have to provide a very small dowry and would not have to feed or host wedding guests! It was settled, a new turban was purchased for Natthu and he headed down to the next wedding fair a few months later to find and marry Sila.

Natthu brought home a chirpy bubbling young girl whose face stayed hidden underneath a long oodhniy whenever she was in public. Jona-ba had hoped that young Sila would become part of the family easily. After all, this is why there was a tradition of marrying off girls while they were still young so it was easier for them to get used to the new family. She hoped Sila would share her responsibilities and become another woman in the house.

But Sila was still a child of fifteen and used every opportunity to remind Natthu that he needed to keep his young bride wife bedecked with colourful oodhniys and melodious glass bangles. Jona-ba remembered her own youth and revelled in the nostalgic reminders of carefree times. But Sila and Natthu were only too eager to establish their family and Johari was born the same year. Despite her worry that it was all too soon, Jona-ba's joys knew no bounds. A girl-child meant a burden for some, but not for her. The beautiful little baby girl would surely usher good changes and Jona-ba now became 'Moti-ba' or elder mother.

Moti-ba's hopes were short lived. Sila was only sixteen when she bore Johari. She missed her own untethered childhood more than the joy of her newly bestowed motherhood. The farmers were being hit hard, there was less and less rain in the region. The long fingers of drought drew deep marks on the soil of the region, and famers began leaving the barren lands to work in the city. When Johari turned ten months, Natthu left to look for work in Amdavad. Sila pined for Natthu and waited each afternoon in the shade of the wada walls, listening for the crunching sound of his footsteps on the dusty village road that lead to Amdavad, covering her eyes against the glare, looking eagerly across every direction, through the scrub and desert, simply hoping for some news. The postman never brought letters for this village nor did any visitors bring news of her husband. She returned each dusk beaten, muddy and parched, until one evening—she did not return. She had followed the mirage of her Natthu one afternoon which lead her away into the dry cold evening. In Lunawa, women who wandered away alone were seldom heard of again. Natthu did not return either.

The men in her life had left Moti-ba. Widowhood had not been kind to Moti-ba. This was once a tall and stately woman. She would take on working in any fields that the farmers could plough, sometimes taking the neighbour's camels, goats or sheep out to graze in exchange for paltry sums of money to make ends meet. With Natthu and Sila gone, having the complete responsibility of Johari changed her life again. She saw Johari as her second chance, a blessing. While infant girls were being secretly killed in Rajasthan and others allowed to succumb to the drought and famine, Moti-ba resolved to ensure Johari survived. She was going to use what little money she had saved to purchase her first water buffalo. The milk would feed the baby and perhaps, she could earn a few extra coins to purchase food for herself. Moti-ba was a strong and determined woman.

Over thirty years of widowhood had curved Moti-ba's back. She had become one with the melancholy colors of her maroon skirt and plain, unbedecked oodhniy, customary for widows. She had long relinquished her jewellery, her nose ring and bangles. Her oodhniy covered her clean-shaved head and remained tucked behind her ears exposing tattooed temples—the only surviving adornment on her body, reminders of times when she was allowed to look beautiful.

At fifty, she was covered in wrinkles, those dark eyes that had captured Dhuni were now sunken into her face, earlobes stretched out long from once having worn heavy earrings, and her once henna covered palms were now callused from working with her growing herd of livestock. She was determined that Johari learnt to sign her name if nothing else, that she would be married into a large and wealthy family with no dearth of resources. She deserved more than the desert had promised her. Moti-ba's mountains of hardships remained dwarfed by her determination. She garnered the respect of her village—her words became her command. Lunawa knew that there was no escaping Moti-ba's word or judgement. She became the only woman allowed to sit alongside the elders at the village council. Sheltered within wada walls and by Moti-ba's word, Johari was the light of her life and of the village—the adored one, the protected one.

That March morning, as Moti-ba crossed over the threshold of her mud hut, out from the shadows of the oty (covered porch) onto the dung smeared open space outside her house, she saw the little boy with his bloodied head, the face of the voice howling "Thieves are here...", tearing through the wada entrance, running haplessly towards her. Her grip on her tamarind stick weakened at first and tightened again. Moti-ba bellowed a decree to the women to go indoors and shut the doors, calling above the fast-approaching commotion. The men were still at the fields but she feared the 'thieves' had got to them too because she did not see anyone return to protect the women. She instructed the boy to return to his mother, he was only a boy.

Flecks of colour appeared in the dust suggesting sashes of multi-coloured clothing. The glints of metal coupled with the sound of gunfire and screams told Moti-ba that these were no ordinary thieves. They were religious fanatics and crusaders looking to kill. Company soldiers were following behind hoping to kerb the violence but were outnumbered. It looked like her people of Lunawa would be next to be caught in the crossfire of the smouldering unrest that had swallowed her love, Dhuni. Although this was not their fight, today it had come to her doorstep. Today it was not just their fight, it was her fight. As the Rao of Sirohi helplessly watched from afar, Lunawa was being ransacked and looted. Moti-ba was not going not let them harm her or Johari. She would stay behind.

Moti-ba had no time to try and shut the wada gates, she felt alone as the women fled indoors to her decree. She quickly called to Johari and dragged her by the hands to the shed to the side of the house, choosing to hide behind hay bales, waiting for the crusaders to pass. They were looking for moneylenders—the famine had made looters of farmers. Johari was shaking in fear and confusion. Moti-ba's water buffaloes were restless too, waving long tails and swatting imaginary flies off their coarse grey backs as they regurgitated cud. Someone called out their names and Moti-ba quickly clasped a hand on Johari's agape mouth and cautioned her.

"Take heart, child, we don't know who is calling."

Until now, Johari had only seen the world through the stories Moti-ba wove for her, through the songs and ballads sung by kawadia bhats, songs of holy men, faithful husbands and pious wives, of handsome, gallant princes and kings. She had only imagined the lives of princes and princesses through the puppets and their abrupt movements governed by a skilled puppeteer who hid behind a colourful curtain. Moti-ba's stories included descriptions of beautifully carved palaces with grand fairs in the beautiful white city of Udaipur, its glistening lakes and painted frescos that she had seen in her youth. Johari had only heard of kingdoms where kings built gardens for their daughters and of the slender maidens sauntering in them, of tales

of brave men and women, of keeping honour and glory alive before submission, and of men who guarded their own. It was the Rajput way.

Today, Johari's visions were replaced with those of revulsion to the sounds she heard, her eyes brimming in disbelief. From their corner in the shed, she could see women and children running helter-skelter, screaming as their homes were being raided. Johari watched in fear as she saw women and children dragged out from their hiding spots, beaten and left to die because they would not part with any money. The defiant shrieks of the looters were followed by loud wails of women. What was this world and who were these people? Moti-ba had not said anything about these vile creatures. Johari's eyes looked searchingly over Moti-ba's wrinkled face, hoping for an answer. As the fires inched closer to them, Moti-ba feared she could not truly protect Johari from these ravaging fanatics. With a heavy heart, only one fear-laden word could spill out from Moti-ba's cracked lips——her words were decree.

"Go."

The ageing matron lay her hand, heavy with hesitation, on Johari's bare head. Johari knew not to question. Honour before submission was their family motto, the motto of the Rajputs and Johari abided Moti-ba's command. She took a quick low bow, in an attempt to touch Moti-ba's feet, but her fingers simply grazed the hem of her skirt. There was no time for ritual, she had to leave now.

But where should Johari go? Until today, her feet were barely scuffed, always staying within the protection of leather mojdis (slippers) or caressing the cool shade of the dung-plastered floors of their house. She had heard of nearby villages but had never stepped out. That trip was saved for her wedding day. Yet, at that moment, mortal fear demanded that she obey Moti-ba's command and run.

In the midst of the rampant confusion, Johari snuck out of the shed and ran towards the fields. She glanced to her left and knew that beyond Sirohi lay the dry desert, from where her mother had never returned. She was not dressed for the desert and there would be no one there. Her simple mirrored skirt was now dragging; it was now torn and dusty. When she had curled it under her feet as she crouched with Moti-ba, she had sullied its demure threadwork. Her clothes were still warm from the kitchen fire, where she had just been preparing their morning meals before she was pulled into this commotion—she was now drenched with trepidation. She had lost her anklets to the haste and forgotten to put on her mojdis. Young girls from good families did not leave the house especially without an oodhniy, but this was all she could be taking with her. The smell of fear clung to her, along with the memory of her family hearth, but nowhere to go. She ran past the fields to the edge of the village— she needed to decide how far she could go today. The scrub vegetation at the edge of the village was not dense but might be enough to shelter her for the night, she thought. She would return the next morning.

Johari fell asleep before sunset. When she woke, the noises had subsided and the sky was aglow with the eerie heat of a burning village. Johari spent the night wondering what would be left of her home, hoping Moti-ba was safe. But dawn brought a difficult sight. From a little perch in the babul tree, Johari saw grey and black smoke colouring the skies above. The crusaders had set fire to the village and burnt everything. There was nothing to walk towards. Johari had to walk away from it.

The shadows of the trees told her that if she headed away from Lunawa, she would be going south. Surely there would be other villages and perhaps kind people. Perhaps Moti-ba had been able to escape and go that way. The railways went down that way too—she would look for the line—perhaps it would lead her to a new place. Scared but determined, she began walking, using a twig of a babul brush to cover her head as she walked and its shade to shelter her when she stopped. The date palms seemed useless from afar, but on two occasions she found a few dates dropped by the monkeys at its base and once, a small stream nearby. She was going to survive this.

She had run away from her village while the crusaders were still on the rampage. After one day of walking in the arid countryside, fear gripped her again; what would she do if they found her? She found the remains of an old Shiva temple and decided to rest there for the day. She hoped the temple would offer protection. Most of it had fallen but the stone structure was cool at night and had a corner with a portion of the roof still intact. In her fear, she did not think about the scorpions that might have been hiding in the cracks. It would be death before surrender. Stacking together a few of the stones from the temple ruins, she reached over and perched herself on a cross-beam holding up the roof—in case the crusaders took shelter there.

At daybreak, Johari realised that the crusaders did not pass that way, that she also had spent two nights un-escorted and away from home. Even if she considered walking back to Lunawa, it was too late to return. She would be marked as a stray loose woman, and it would be worse if Moti-ba was not there to stand up for her. If Moti-ba was not there, who would believe her? Would she find anyone left? Johari had to continue onward to find the next village. She walked for many hours, resting in abandoned temples or in trees until she felt she was far enough.

Johari reached the village of Lanva one afternoon, three days after she had left Lunawa. Little did she know that she had crossed into the next state, Gujarat, but though there was a state line, Lanva was not unlike her own little village Lunawa. Tall medas (look out posts) kept watch on the outside along the wada wall and the wada gate was just like the one in Lunawa. Village matrons took turns to keep a watch on the comings and goings of its residents as well as strangers who ventured its way. No male outsider was allowed in without permission. Johari was comforted by the familiarity—this might be close to home, perhaps they would accept her into their fold. The sight of a young girl entering their wada in the heat of the afternoon, without her oodhniy or mojdi, covered in the dust of the desert set the women to task—their quiet afternoon had just found purpose. One of the women brought her water and another fetched a weak chaas (buttermilk), the heat could be brutal. The more Johari spoke, the more they gasped and consoled her. They had heard of an old woman in Lunawa, one who was once Jona-ba. This was hopeful, Johari thought. This seemed like a place of refuge. One of the old women of the village had met Jona-ba in her youth. Johari was comforted at the connection she made with the old woman, hopeful that her grandmother might still be alive and safe somewhere. She would ask the elders if someone could help look for her.

But there was no escaping the tales of horror of the aftermath of the attack on Lunawa. Passersby and visitors brought stories of the massacre to the Lanva village folks lives. Some stories were less gruesome than some claimed, but at other times magnified. Johari had her own tale of slaughter and death, and of Moti-ba. As the days passed, travellers verified the horrific tragedy of Lunawa, there was no one or nothing left. There was no word of even the old matron, Moti-ba. In place of what once was a village were large blackened ruins of what used to be homes and lives.

But the destruction of one village presented a new dilemma to this village— what was to become of this young refugee girl? The men folk, young and old, had already begun to lustfully eye her. What if Johari was of loose character and had made up all the stories of the atrocities?

They had to safeguard their own moral code but the tongues wagged. The village well became increasingly abuzz with gossip and doubt, as the women magnified her tales more and more. Each time someone passed her, Johari became stripped of her own identity. She was now the abandoned girl, who needed shelter and sympathy, not an ambiguous halfway house in Lanwa. The prospect of her unknown moral character having an unforeseen, disastrous influence on the yet unmarried girls of their village worried the village council. They decided if a suitable man from the village found her desirable, he should marry her, or else Johari should move on and out to the next village, another few days walk away.

The old matrons of the village pointed in the direction of Sonaji, the simpleton son of an old widow, Chamu-ba. Although of a marriageable age, he had not found a suitable wife for himself and talk of his absentminded nature had kerbed any possible proposals coming his way. He was a simple farmer who was often found wandering empty fields after a day's work, feeding his mid-day meals to the peacocks and peahens or spending days without speaking a word to anyone. But he was a good man. It was about time he was married. There was no reason to wait for the next wedding fair. When Johari heard of this match, she had no opinion of her own. This was one way she could stay safe. The old woman who had taken her in convinced her that this was the right thing to do. She would not have the wedding finery her grandmother had promised her, nor a plush wedding to a rich merchant—Johari had no choice. After a simple exchange of garlands and the customary dedication to the ceremonial fire, Johari and Sonaji were tied in the age-old tradition of matrimony.

While Johari ached for Moti-ba's blessings at her wedding and beyond and resented the denial of her dreams, Sonaji did not see matrimony as a reason to change his routine. He continued to head out to the fields at the break of dawn, sometimes even when the fields were bare. They were hoping for rain that year. Johari would take him his lunch, most often a bajra rotlo or a jowar rotlo, with some raw onions or a garlic chutney, just before the heat of the sun began to scorch her feet. She often sat in the shade of the babul trees while Sonaji fell asleep on the madi, looking for peacock feathers or counting how many parrots flew between trees. She would head back when the shadows arched away from her again, when the sandy dust was just bearable on the soles of her feet.

Johari was still just a child, growing up all by herself. It was impossible to replace the warm and authoritative mother-figure, Moti-ba, but Chamu-ba slid into the spot by default. Still fighting the absence of her dear grandmother, Johari began her married life in physical and emotional isolation. She had been home, less than a month ago, and was still only 14. It was still 1899, and the Kawadia bhatt, the puppeteer, had lied.

CHAPTER TWO

A Runaway

1900-: LANVA, GUJARAT

Slowly but surely, Johari settled into being a married woman. Despite her latent resistance, Chamu-ba managed to teach Johari how to take care of the home, their cattle, and of course, Sonaji. Moti-ba had taught her to cook some of the essential meals but she had intended for Johari to marry rich. She was not to be the wife of an absentminded farmer, with a small house and a herd of cattle. Sonaji remained the aloof simpleton, wandering off into the fields at will, doing his mother's bidding and sleeping when he knew his tasks were done. He was not a worldly man but he was a good man. He worked hard, made sure there was food and clothing for his family, and never once touched liquor. Johari was the one who stood up for the family, who made the tough decisions. In due time Sonaji's affection towards Johari grew. Eight years after they were married, Johari bore a son, Thakor. Three years after Thakor came Suraj, Johari's second son, the apple of her eye.

Johari raised her children on stories of her own grandmother, Moti-ba. Her strength came in reliving those memories and her eyes glistened in pride and sorrow, recalling the day she had to leave her own home. Suraj was simply content to sit in Johari's lap, staying in Thakor's shadows, revelling in Chamu-ba's affections——he was the baby of the house, he aimed for no more. But Thakor saw more in his mother's stories——he saw her fears and her hopes——he caught a glimpse of her smiles when she talked about her youth——all before she came to Lanva. He could sense her emotions through her warm hands when she fed him, or when she straightened his tunic some mornings on his way to school. Each year he became more determined, headstrong like her Moti-ba, eager to make his own mother proud, making fervent attempts to nudge his way into his mother's affections.

Each morning, Thakor would head to the village school, to sit at the very front of the class, so he could learn. Perhaps, he would be able to teach his mother to read and write and fulfill his great-grandmother's dreams for her. But despite his best intentions, the boy's efforts were never rewarded. Johari had known that Moti-ba had wanted her to learn to read and write, so she always remained eager to find a willing teacher. Of course, the only one who came forward was Thakor when he started attending school when he turned ten. But Thakor realised quickly that at home, he would be contending with Suraj's pleas for attention, and at school, there was Bhagat.

Bhagat Pandit was the son of the headmaster Haribhai Pandit, a man who wore many hats. The privileged headmaster came from a family of priests and had been taught to read and write scriptures at an early age. A local Company sahib promised him that if he was able to start a school and teach at least thirty students each year, he would consider building him a one-room official school and name it after him for his noble efforts. The temptation of public glory for an ordinary priest was too much to resist. Running a school was a prestigious task and would also mean extra income for the Pandit family, especially if he was to get a small commission from the Company for it. Haribhai Pandit eagerly replaced the tattered scriptures on his little desk with new books, and was transformed nearly overnight into Masterji, the village headmaster. He found a suitable classroom-like space; the large shady peepal tree just outside the Lanva wada would suffice—its mud floor underneath was plastered with cow dung for the students to sit on—this was good enough. He performed a small pooja underneath the tree, now christened the Tree of Knowledge. Auspicious prayers were recited and bright red kumkum powder and turmeric was generously smeared on its trunk to sanctify the previously ignored tree. A picture frame of Goddess Saraswati was procured, a small garland hung on it and a small rope bed with a mattress and bolster appeared. The Masterji's school was in session, determined to impart the boys of Lanva with just enough knowledge to help them collect dues in the future, from their prosperous lives of being milkmen, farmers, traders and grocers and seek beautiful brides and bountiful dowries from wealthy fathers eager to wed their daughters to educated men.

Masterji had decided to teach the young men of Lanva elementary mathematics and reading. After a few weeks of coaxing, he was able to enlist fourteen students. He was hopeful that more would come, even if they were from nearby villages. His goal was to keep them and for that, he enlisted his oldest son Bhagat to 'inspire' the boys. Any student who answered Masterji's question correctly was able to move up one row until they got to the coveted front row. Only a head shorter than Thakor but twice as big in bulk, Bhagat would be the first to answer a question, the first to watch the class when Masterji needed to take a break from the boys, and of course, the first to bully his classmates when his father was not looking. The kind hearted Thakor was his favourite prey.

Each day Thakor headed to school on time to secure a spot at the front of the class. Bhagat would find a chore and send him back to the village to retrieve something or the other for Masterji and invariably cause Thakor to be late. The only way he could move up during class was if he answered all the questions correctly. But as luck would have it, he never made it farther up than the second row. This went on for two years, and Thakor had figured out that his chances of advancing in the class were slim.

One day, Thakor grudgingly made his way to school, dragging his feet knowing he would only get to sit in the back, and there was no reason to arrive early. Masterji had begun teaching them poetry and verse, and would often slip into his priestly role and chant hymns, only to trigger a bout of yawns and drooping eyes as the boys tried to stay awake in the mid-morning sunshine. When he reached, he found Bhagat absent, he was sick that day. Delighted, he claimed a spot in the front and continued through. Masterji noticed Thakor's enthusiasm that day, and before long, began favouring him in class. Bhagat's illness was short-lived especially when he discovered that his spot at the top of the class was being challenged and his father had found a willing and eager learner. One evening after school was out, Masterji asked Thakor to stay back and help him. Word was sent to Johari-ba that Thakor would be late. Bhagat had a plan.

Bhagat could dare not miss this opportunity to reset the balance of power in his domain. He decided to lay in wait under a tamarind tree while the rest of his classmates headed home. Thakor was brimming with pride as he headed home eager to tell his Ba how much Masterji had taught him that day. His pace only quickened as he saw Bhagat, knowing that good-for-nothing was up to causing trouble. Bhagat was not alone, he had two accomplices. He stood tauntingly, challenging Thakor to a duel to prove his worth, for the true worth of a man was when he was book-smart and street-smart! Sticks and fists appeared in quick succession in the hands of Bhagat and his friends. They had challenged him to a fight.

Thakor was outnumbered but determined not be overpowered. He was raised on fresh water-buffalo milk straight from the buffalo's udder, hearty rotlas, and his favourite, laapsi. Johari-ba would make laapsi only on special days; it would be submerged under a heavy layer of liquid gold—home-made ghee. Thakor's mind wandered momentarily at the thought of the delicious treat but a hit on his back shook him back to the now. There was no chance he was going to let Ba down! Blow after blow followed and very soon the four boys were covered in blood and dust. Someone lost his turban, Thakor's books were scattered in the dirt, Bhagat and his friends were going to teach this boy a lesson. There were times when Thakor did not know whose twisted arms and hands were attacking him, so he simply hit and punched without a thought. He was not going to let these bullies take him down. Finally, his hands landed on a stick. One of the boys had dropped it.

One of the boys had aimed for his head, and hit him in the eye instead. The throbbing pain was distracting him, so he had to keep that eye shut. Covering his eye with a cupped palm, he grabbed the stick and swung it around blindly, yelling at the top of his lungs, hoping to hit someone, and it did. Thakor heard a loud crack and in an instant, the scuffling ceased. A body crumpled through the dust and fell towards Thakor. The boy fell on his cheek, it was Bhagat, blood gushing out from his temple and his open jaw. Thakor's blow had knocked him out cold. No one knew what to say, Bhagat's friends stepped backwards, stumbling over their own partially unravelled dhotis, until they decided to abandon the scene and run back home, screaming.

It took a few minutes for Thakor to realise what had just happened. There was warm blood trickling down from his temple and clouding his eye, his hands ached, his palms were numb, and in front of him lay a figure much like him, just senseless. He bent over and tried to shake Bhagat awake, but the boy just moaned in pain. Relieved that Bhagat was alive, Thakor wondered what would happen next. Should he go to the village and seek help? No, Bhagat's friends would do that. What would happen when Ba found out? She would not spare him. She would reach for the broom and beat him. He recalled the sting of the dried and barbed branches of the broom on his skin when she had punished him once before; she had even added prickly babul branches to her broom for added emphasis. But the sting of his mother's beating would not compare to the hurt and anger he would see in her eyes. Johari-ba was a proud woman, she would rather disown him than punish him for an act so unforgiving. Thakor knew that Bhagat would live but he could not bear to see his mother's disappointment in him. While one dust storm of Bhagat's friends headed to the village, another plume formed as Thakor ran to hide in the fields. Suraj would not miss him and Bapu (father) would not care much. He only worried about Ba and what she would think—he did not want to go back home to be reprimanded just yet.

Trying to get away from the mayhem, Thakor headed towards the bajra fields, they would make a fine hiding place till daybreak. He started off, running at first, and then walking until he found himself surrounded by the tall and beautiful ivory heads of bajra. The stunning crop was the pride of their village, just about ready for harvest in a few weeks. The fields were swaying, the bajra heads dancing at the slightest breeze. The peaceful sight calmed Thakor's nerves momentarily. He found Bapu's favourite sleeping spot, the raised platform. He climbed up and tried to sleep. But his sleep was disturbed. He could hear the shrill calls of peacocks to their mates; Thakor imagined them to be the sounds of shrieking demons. Dusk became night, and the October mist rose over the fields. He saw the moonrise and thought, another few days until the Purnima (full moon) celebrations. But the shadows of the trees started taking on unusual shapes. The bajra heads resembled spears marching towards him, he crouched in fear. As the mist rose and curled, it mingled with the smell of burning wood and the smoke emanating from small cooking stoves of the homes in his village. Thakor was starting to regret his decision to run away and hide. Ba might be making hot rotlas for everyone, he thought. He missed being home, he missed being warm. The howling jackals did not soothe his fears and before long, Thakor was frustrated, scared and disappointed that no one had come looking for him, not even Bapu!

Thakor was imagining dragons and snakes in those sinuous shapes of the mist; the winds blowing over the fields made it look like hordes of people were marching towards him. The village had never been short of ghost stories and Thakor's thoughts wandered towards their seductive intrigue. What if the ghosts were real? If he waited and watched the ghosts, and lived, he would forever be known as the brave boy who saw the ghosts. But what if a ghost came to possess him? He had heard that they were attracted by the smell of fresh blood! Thakor looked down at his wounds and panicked; he had to get out of there.

Scrambling down from the raised platform, Thakor carefully made his way out of the fields. Once he found a dirt path, he felt better but the shapes of the shadows bothered him, followed him, they never seemed to leave. There was the story of a haggard old daakan (witch) who tricked and possessed strays if they walked past her banyan tree near the village lake—he would have to avoid that route. He found a stick and started walking faster and faster on a path he knew would take him to Mehsana. It would be a few hours-worth of a walk, but he was sure that is where he wanted to go. He would come back to Ba and Bapu another day. Lanva was not the place for him right now. There was a new rail line to Amdavad. At four in the morning, the next day, there would be a twelve-year-old ticketless passenger at the train station of Mehsana, waiting to board a train to Amdavad. He would find a job and come back home when he had made something of himself.

The ticket checker was working the Amdavad bound train. He had boarded a few stations before Mehsana, at Palanpur, just before it was dawn—this would be a long day, he thought. The train was going to stop at Mehsana only briefly that morning; there were only a few passengers. Sauntering through the swaying compartments, he reached the one where some of the Mehsana passengers had boarded. He saw a dust-covered boy, head down, arms crossed over his chest and hunched near the window of the compartment— this fellow will not have a ticket. He tapped the boy's shoulder with a well-rehearsed questioning expression, making a clucking sound in his cheek.

But when Thakor looked up, the ticket collector saw a bloodied temple, a bruised cheek and the bright white of one eye staring back at him. The ticket collector's jaw dropped open in surprise.

"Ma Ambe (Mother Goddess)! What happened to you? Do you have a ticket?"

His dialect was a mix of Hindi, Rajasthani, and Gujarati, typical of the area. Thakor felt no reason to explain himself but answered the last question by curling in even more, tightening his posture and sitting upright, shaking his head vigorously in a mute "no". There was something about the boy's eyes—he was angry, scared, and looked terribly hungry. There was a sacred black thread on his neck, an initialled tattoo at the base of his left thumb and his wrist was wrapped in a tattered and faded yellow and orange token 'blessing-thread' from a temple. The blood from his temple had dripped onto his shirt and had dried into a shade of brown. This was no ordinary runaway; he seemed to have a family. It took only a few words of chatting to learn that the boy was from Lanva, the village where his sister had been married a few years ago, to none other than Haribhai Panditji's nephew.

The new-found familiarity changed the ticket checker's authoritative stance—it quickly took a back seat to pity, he stopped the interrogation and a little smirk graced his face. Young boys tend to be hot headed, he had seen it far too often; and this one was not unlike most boys who run away. He chatted for a few minutes and let him be, returning to check on him just before Amdavad. He bought Thakor a cup of cha (tea) and some onion bhajiya (fritters) from a vendor at the railway station, the vendor not much older than Thakor himself. The spicy chutney with the bhajiya was sharp and jolted his taste buds. He also thrust a few coins of loose change in Thakor's palm—to find a doctor while he was in Amdavad who could tend to his wound. He chuckled, saying he could pay him back when he visited Lanva, reminding Thakor to return home after he had come to his senses and that this was an ill-planned rebellion of running away. The train from Amdavad back to Mehsana was not until the next morning; he could ride back without a ticket if they were on the same train together. Besides, Amdavad had some nice temples and a beautiful lake; perhaps Thakor could make a trip out of it after all.

Although grateful for the kindness, food, and money, Thakor had no intentions of returning to Mehsana just yet, let alone a sightseeing trip in Amdavad. He paced the train station, pretending to take the ticket collector's advice, but was biding his time until his generous new friend left. Amdavad looked like a town filled with unusual buildings—what he learned later to be a mix between Muslim homes and traditional Hindu homes and temples. The men and women who came to the platform did not look like people from his village. Some women were dressed in long coats and many men wore tiny, boat-shaped hats instead of turbans. Ba's stories had taught him to be cautious. This town had swallowed his grandfather. Thakor felt out of place.

The cha and bhajiyas temporarily energised Thakor, and he paced about trying to come up with a plan. He had walked the train station several times, sitting on a bench here, resting on his haunches elsewhere, until a constable became suspicious. Thakor gave the constable a smile and a nod, found a bench and sat down. He counted the coins from the morning, they amounted to a little less than sixteen anna's, less than one rupee. But it was a generous loan. Thakor knew he would not return to Lanva just yet, perhaps some time in the future. He was going to use the money for something else. It would buy him a few morsels, but it was not enough seed money for the runaway. Perhaps Mumbai (Bombay) would have something better for him. Thakor boarded the next train to Mumbai, again without a ticket, avoiding the ticket collector by hiding under the seat when he was not looking.

Thakor reached Mumbai three days after having left Lanwa—getting off at the Victoria Terminus, the last train station on this train line. This city smelt different, the air was salty and humid, he was sweating. People were rushing around like they had to get somewhere. He got out and looked around—the station was made of carved black volcanic rock abundant in the region; with strange and sometimes scary demon-like figures peering at him. The tall arched halls of the train station were grand, but he felt more scared than impressed.

Right outside the train station was a large street. This was a new view. There were more buildings around him with arched walkways and peering animals; perhaps it was a popular look around here, he thought. It was green and lush with lots of trees. There were horse-drawn carts taking people around and bullock carts transporting goods. He saw a Company sahib sitting comfortably in a hand-drawn cart pulled by a middle-aged shirtless man wearing a large white turban and a dhoti, dropping beads of sweat as he jogged along. There were Company soldiers milling at a distance, and young boys not much older than him, dressed in dhotis and jackets, playing mischief on their older teacher who was reprimanding them for something as he led them across the street. "All masterjis are alike," he muttered. The people were dressed different than him, but Thakor found humour and comfort in the scene.

Perhaps this town could use another hard worker like him, and Thakor began walking, hoping to find work somewhere in this city.

Meanwhile, back in Lanva, Johari-ba heard of the scuffle, how her son had beaten the Masterji's boy until he almost died. She was mortified but knew that her Thakor had the heart of a kind lion—he would retaliate only if he was in trouble. She refused to believe that he had done any wrong. She challenged the village council that if he returned, she would bring him to them, and let him face justice. She secretly hoped he would not. The days became months, festivals came and went, three harvests were sown and reaped—Thakor had not returned.

Johari-ba continued her life in the village, tending to her water buffaloes, pandering to Suraj's demands, taking care of her absentminded Sonaji and his ageing mother Chamu-ba, who had now fully given into sitting at the steps of the temple and helping Panditji with his daily prayers. When Suraj turned fifteen, Chamu-ba expressed the desire to take a pilgrimage along with her prayer group; Sonaji offered to accompany them. Suraj was supposed to continue his school work at Masterji's school, now a legitimate establishment. Their pilgrimage would take a few months to complete. Two months into the pilgrimage, the first postcard arrived. The group had finally reached the shores of the mighty Ganga River at Rishikesh but were not able to continue further. Chamu-ba had slipped while taking a bath in the raging holy waters and could not walk anymore. They needed to stay on a little longer to see if her condition improved; Sonaji was to take care of his mother, and with the words "By the grace of God" ended the postcard. Johari-ba let out a little sigh—Sonaji would not be back for the harvest again this year; they would need to seek the help of the villagers again.

Johari-ba's latest predicament became the talk of the wada; but with Masterji frequently reminding anyone who would listen of the absconding Thakor, no one came to help her. There were only two homes in Lanva with extra time on their hands: Masterji's family and Udham Darjee, the village tailor's—his family had three young lads to spare after they had tended to their own five fields. The village folk of Lanva were only allowed to wear clothes sewn by someone from within their village, and between farming and sewing, the Darjee family was always busy around the festivals but not as much the rest of the year.

Sarayu knew first-hand what it meant to rely on their neighbours to give them any business or help. Johari-ba and Sarayu had been kind to each other; Johari-ba also found solidarity in Sarayu, who felt sorry for her situation. She offered a few hours of help each day until her harvest was completed, in exchange for three bags of the harvest. The bags of jowar and bajra from Johari-ba's fields only strengthened the friendship.

Johari-ba received an occasional postcard from Sonaji in the first year; the postman read it to her on her stoop. Each said the same things. Chamu-ba had been unable to walk, her health was getting worse and the two of them were staying on at the ashram in Rishikesh. Everyone else in that pilgrimage group had returned, Johari-ba had stopped caring. One year passed and then two, until one afternoon when Johari found Sonaji at her doorstep, tired and sweaty, asking for a drink of water. Johari-ba's relief knew no bounds until she found he had returned alone.

His last postcard had come three months ago. A month after that, Chamu-ba had passed away peacefully in her sleep, right after they had returned from listening to the evening bhajan and prayers at the Ganga-ji Ghaat, the steps along the banks of the Ganges River. Sonaji had no choice but to complete her final rites there itself, and in his grief had denounced his family and all. His feet had led him home because he had no place else to go. But his mind was as barren as the fallowed fields after the last harvest. There was nothing left.

Johari-ba was now responsible for two men who saw little merit in making themselves useful. Suraj would spend hours in the fields and finish only a fraction of what he was expected to. He was always asking Johari-ba for money, to go to the fair, to go to the market, or perhaps buy a wad of tobacco. He even started hinting that he wanted to get married—Johari-ba simply scowled, reminding him that he needed to do more before she was willing to bring another person into the home. She had come to this village alone and was now living in it alone. She had no place else to go but was surely not going to trap another young girl in this God-forsaken family.

She missed Thakor, her son with a heart-of-gold, who would write to her every few months. The postman and Sarayu were her only confidants about his postcards, lest the village rose up in arms against the absconding boy. Thakor was in the great and grand city of Mumbai. Two years after his first postcard, came a small money order for five rupees. It was a lot of money! She knew that he had been working someplace, there was a return address on his postcards, but Thakor did not write more. The address began as 'Care Of' or c/o. Perhaps some kind family had taken him in? She was grateful that at least one of her sons cared enough for her, and sent her money.

With every postcard, Johari-ba would feel the urge to write back. She would even ask the postman to ready his pen. But there was nothing new or exciting to write to him about. Did she really want to tell him that she felt alone and abandoned? Did she want to tell him that his father had denounced the family, that his brother had turned into the village bum, or that his grandmother had passed on? There was no need to share this kind of sadness. The boy was obviously working hard and earning a living. She prayed that he was not involved in any wrong doing. And she promised herself and the postman that she would write when there was better news to share.

Johari-ba would pay Sarayu to help her out in the fields with the money that Thakor sent her. She saved Thakor's postcards, even though she could not read them. Suraj found out about his mother's source of money and used it to his advantage. His life was now painted and plentiful, thanks to Thakor's hard work and his mother's guilt.

Sarayu understood Johari-ba's suffering. She was spending more and more time with her, and would remind anyone willing to listen, that Johari-ba had experienced her fair share of tragedy in life. She had earned her respect by suffering through it all. Johari-ba was grateful and started to see her family as an extension of her own. Sarayu's sons were kind and respectful, and they adored her, especially, Pratap, the youngest one. He would have done anything for her and she felt the same motherly affection towards him. How she wished Suraj would learn something from Pratap, but it was not meant to be.

One afternoon, Sarayu and Johari-ba sat in the shade of the stoop of Johari's hut—this was their time to be mothers and friends together while the men were in the fields. They could watch over the wada from its shade. The women were planning a visit to Durga Mata-ji's temple for the upcoming festival of Navratri. One of the girls wanted Sarayu to teach her how to embroider. Some girls played gutte' with pebbles, a simple game of tossing one pebble in the air and collecting the remaining with their other hand. Another group of girls sat braiding each other's hair. It was a normal afternoon at the wada; the wind was warm and the shadows harsh but the sight of women scattered unhindered around the wada was comforting. Johari-ba looked up abruptly, she heard the bleating of startled goats. The goat herders were not expected back for a bit, she wondered what the commotion could possibly be. Her eyes glazed above the edge of the wada walls only to spot a line of dust approaching their village. She barely had a minute to steady herself and approach the wada entrance, when a platoon of horse-mounted Company sepoys made their way into the enclave. Not only was their presence in the area unusual, they had dared to enter the enclave where outsiders were not allowed without permission. This startled the women, their afternoon routine disrupted, as they scurried about to first cover their heads and faces with their oodhniy, and then to find the shade and protection of their own homes.

Their unannounced arrival triggered memories of the last time sepoys entered Johari's village. She walked out angrily towards them. The company was led by a Gora-sahib (uniformed white man) wearing a large, funny looking hat with a plume of feathers. He was in uniform, as was the rest of his company. There were only women in the wada right now. She insisted they apologise and leave, and seek permission to enter their village when the men had returned from the fields. Standing tall, head held high, she had an air of authority to her. But no woman had ever challenged a Gora-sahib, this was simply not done in this part of Gujarat.

The dry desert breeze froze momentarily and a sudden vacuum engulfed everyone in horrified silence. Only the sound of the restless hooves and bleating of startled goats punctuated the unsettling quiet. This was not a good sign.

The officer puffed out his chest and let out a loud sigh, declaring he was on Company business, he could go wherever he pleased. They were looking for a gaddar (a defector) but he would be happy to arrest her in his place if she continued to resist their presence. He disembarked, hoping to allow her to fully appreciate the purpose of his arrival. But Johari-ba saw this as a direct threat. She questioned him again, telling him that the women had not been warned, this was a violation of their privacy, and that the Company should have sought proper permissions. The Gora-sahib was a high-ranking official, and would not be spoken to in this manner by an uneducated woman. Raising his voice, he warned her, that she had already tested his patience. Johari-ba would not have anyone challenging the safety of her home, and her fists tightened in rage as she tucked her oodhniy into her skirt and charged towards the sahib. She grabbed what she could on the way—she had found a stick—with a single swift blow, she hit the officer squarely over his funny plumed hat.

Thwack!

The loud sound broke the stillness of the standoff. Sepoys charged towards her, while women covered their mouths with the ends of their oodhniys as they shared a communal gasp. The man tumbled to his knees, and his company quickly gathered around to arrest Johari-ba. Within minutes Johari-ba's hands were tied up and she was being led to Mehsana to the women's prison. There were no able-bodied men around to protest or stop them. Sonaji had wandered off into the fields again that morning, there was no telling if he would return. Suraj was in Dhinoj that morning with friends and was not likely to return until later in the day.

The sentence for attacking a company officer was six months of jail time. Bail was set at five hundred rupees, a king's ransom for anyone from Lanva. Johari-ba would grind salt by hand, eight hours a day until her prison sentence was over. Any form of rebellion was to be quashed at its roots. They intended to make an example of that impertinent woman.

That evening the elders of Lanva sat down to a panchayat (village elders' council). There were many in Lanva who felt relieved to be rid of a 'trouble-maker', but Sarayu had known a different side of the same woman—she was her friend, a sister. She offered to mortgage her family's own fields to the village, in exchange for five hundred rupees for the bail. Her sons were not the best farmers and they were doing well for themselves as tailors. Udham preferred not to work in the fields, and with her needlework skills they could earn back the money in a few years and get their fields back. She would be happy to go to Mehsana and bail out Johari-ba herself.

The weight of her offer shifted the balance of authority of the panchayat. Their turbaned heads came together and parted as they deliberated how to respond. If they did nothing, it would reflect poorly on the village, and no one would marry into or out of the village. If they did anything, they would be condoning her actions and her Thakur's behaviour. Masterji was not going to let them forget. In that moment, Lanva's women who had witnessed the event in flesh wondered what would have happened if the Gora-sahib had done them harm.

After a span of inaudible murmuring and hushed voices, the panchayat took the decision. They would accept Sarayu's offer. Lanva decided to bury their ego, recognising that Sarayu's sacrifice spoke volumes about their friendship, about the mettle of a person, and that Johari-ba had done so to protect their own village. She had been an outsider once, and they had taken her in. She had the courage to stand up for the women and girls of her village, even though none was her own flesh or blood; she had tried to pay them back in her own way. How could they punish her for having a sense of ownership? They conceded and Lanva came together—it took a little more than a month to put the money in place. Young Pratap and Sarayu lead the elders of Lanva to rescue the pride of their village, the valiant Johari-ba, to bring her home where she truly belonged, while Sonaji spent yet another afternoon wandering the fields.

Chapter Three

Narmada's Waters

1920, Indore, Madhya Pradesh

Ratanlal was born as Ramaji in Rajasthan, and had come to Indore as a young man in the 1910's. He wanted to start afresh so he began by changing his name—to Ratanlal Jadhav. Indore was then a territory governed by the Marathas, a dry interior region but one of regal pomp and splendour. He had been his father's apprentice in one of the princely states of Rajasthan, helping at his pedhi (office), lending money and choosing precious gems for the people who served in the princely courts. They were also budding philanthropists, donating money to worthy causes, temples, and schools. So, when he came to Indore, he found his way to serve the members of the court of the Holkars, the reigning royal family of the region. In a town with its fair share of royalty who loved owning precious gems and jewellery, having the skill to differentiate a piece of coloured glass from a precious stone was tricky but always profitable. Ratanlal felt at ease.

Being in the business of gems meant that sometimes the buyers became sellers, looking to cash out a gaudy large ring or broach for sums of money. Sometimes there were anonymous sellers and anonymous buyers, and Ratanlal quickly learnt to keep the information to himself. In courting wealthy buyers, Ratanlal also developed a penchant for the finer things in life that attracted his clients: foreign whisky, delicately cooked meats, cigars, and horse riding. His sharp wit and skill along with his intricate knowledge of fine jewellery also made him very attractive to young maidens in town. He was a handsome man who understood the way to a woman's heart.

But Ratanlal only had eyes for Shanta, a petite maiden who lived across from his own pedhi—the young girl who peered from the shadows of her second-floor window when she thought he was not looking. If the shutters were open, he might see her. He was waiting until he had come into his own, to ask for her hand in marriage.

One morning, word got around that the Holkars' treasury had been looted dry—there had been a theft in the palace. All eyes steered towards the jewellers and merchants in town, anyone who may have been privy to the knowledge of their worth. They were questioning all who had been near the treasury in the past year, and suspicions began to fly. Perhaps the charismatic young man Ratanlal, the boy who was once a stranger, was not to be trusted. Perhaps he was hoping to get rich there was a decree that his quarters should be searched. A covert battalion headed to the Jadhav Pedhi.

But a man who knew secrets and how to keep them had a few tricks up his sleeve too. Ratanlal had trained a batch of young informants, who served as his eyes and ears in the bylanes of Indore. They scurried over to him, ahead of the battalion to warn him. There was no time, he had to leave. If he was ever taken in for questioning, there was no knowing if he would return. He had not stolen anything, but he had so many precious gems and pieces of jewellery on him, who would believe him? The Holkars may be understanding but they might be looking for revenge? They had the Company on their side. He could not take a chance.

Shanta had been braiding her hair in her room when the untimely commotion of chattering miscreants at Ratanlal's door attracted her attention. She reached out through the bars of the window to open the shutters some more and glanced down to check. She saw a group of boys at Ratanlal's door and rushed down to the stoop to get a closer look. She caught herself before she stepped out—mother had not given her permission to cross the threshold today—her mother did not know, so she hid behind the front door.

Unfolding in front of Shanta was a scene from her worst nightmares. It appeared that Ratanlal was leaving in a hurry. Shanta stood rooted to the spot. This was unusual, what was wrong? Why such a hullabaloo, and where was Ratanlal heading? Would she see him again? They had never exchanged a word in all these years.

Shanta was witnessing the commotion at the Jadhav pedhi. Ratanlal was rushing around, hastily grabbing the sheets covering the floor mattress near his desk and piling it with important belongings—his collateral. In one stack he dumped a few large silver utensils, in the second one he tossed in a few small pouches of perhaps jewellery and a few of his tunic's hanging nearby. He grabbed his turban and a cumberband from a peg on the wall, and tucked in a small pouch and a small dagger as he dressed hurriedly. Loading these two large bindles on to his horse, Ratanlal instructed the boys to cover for him—he was ready to leave. There was no need to return, his belongings would tide him through whatever was to come. Ratanlal slipped on his leather chappals (slippers) and began straddling his horse.

As he started leaving, Ratanlal glanced over at the usual place for one last look—the second-floor window across the street where he was expecting to see Shanta. His brow furrowed, she was not there. He let out a disappointed sigh, and let his gaze swoop below. He saw Shanta's shadow on the grey stone floor of her house, shaped by a thin sliver of light that had pierced the hinges of her front door. She was trying not to be seen, but in her eagerness to not miss one last look, had arched her head out.

This could not be the last time they saw each other. He rode over, across the street, meaning to pause for just a moment, to get a closer look before he left. As he approached, a solitary thought raced through Shanta's mind—she had to speak, but what would she say? Could she stop him? It was bad luck to ask a traveller where he was headed, so she wondered what she would say. Shanta was confused but her feet boldly led her out of the shadows into the doorway where he could see her, and from her lips fell a simple phrase:

"Are you leaving me behind, Rao (sir)?"

Her face lit up as she spoke because she felt brave. The rider was stunned, and his horse was restless to leave. How could Ratanlal leave this fearless woman behind? He had wanted to marry her, but he might not be coming back. What about seeking the right permissions from her family? There was no time for formalities.

Without a word, Ratanlal dismounted and gave a quick bow to his lady. He extended a hand out to Shanta, helping her saddle his horse and mounted behind her right away. She was petite and nimble—the horse would be able to take on two riders. He took a deep breath as Shanta settled over the horse's saddle, kicked his heels and rode out of town.

Shanta did not know where she was heading, and neither did Ratanlal. They were strangers to each other, having merely exchanged glances all these years, now tied together in a journey. Shanta had walked away from her home with only the clothes on her back, but her honour was in his hands. The two riders headed out and away from Indore. Shanta comforted in knowing that Ratanlal was skilled and smart, and yet was fearful of her fate. Ratanlal wondered how far he would have to ride before he could feel safe. His foremost task was to get away from there.

They rode until dusk without food or water and reached the banks of the Narmada River at Maheshwar, the horse was tired and so were the riders, they needed to stop. Maheshwar was a little town filled with temples, well known for its skilled weavers. It was another Holkar stronghold that Ratanlal had visited once before to trade. But he had not visited like this, stealthily, as though he had something to hide. He had to make sure they were safe, perhaps a rested night here would help them plan ahead.

But each passing moment reminded Ratanlal that Shanta was with him, an unmarried maiden. Her honour and virtue would remain at stake if a night passed between them and they continued to ride with together. Not knowing what to do next, he first purchased two simple nav-wari (nine-yard) sarees for Shanta. The naïve girl had hastily joined him without a change of clothes! The sarees were not ornate— they needed to be simple—they could not attract attention. They headed to the Narmada ghaat along the bank of the river for the evening. He tied his horse to a post outside the entrance to the ghaat and they walked towards the river, dragging their two bindles with them.

The gentle waters of the Narmada lapped at the base of the ghaats, simple stone steps lead down to the river, its soft clapping sounds were soothing. They would have to rest here for the night. Ratanlal knew that devotees would not return until the next dawn for their ritualistic dip in the river before sunrise. Ratanlal assumed resting in plain view would also protect Shanta's honor. They could take the shelter under the cloak of the night sky, and Shanta could leave if she changed her mind about eloping with him.

As the sun began to set, Ratanlal and Shanta walked down the stone steps and sat by a small Shivling, a shrine to Lord Shiva. There was a larger temple nearby, but they were not ready to answer the questions of its priests just yet. The Shivling overlooked the calm Narmada River. This tiny shrine was not placed inside a temple or under a canopy like in most other temples but was just there, a reminder of the omnipresent, boundless sacred, of God. Shanta sat next to it, her feet folded to one side, her arm supporting her body weight, head covered by the end of her saree, crouching next to Ratanlal. They looked into the sunset and wondering what would be next for them.

The Narmada flowed east to west and the sunset lit up the waters shades of gold and orange, mesmerising anyone who watched it flow. It was a holy river, and devotees thronged to it at festivals. But today was a quiet evening and barring a few devout Hindus reciting evening prayers, Shanta and Ratanlal were alone.

A devotee had just taken a dip in the cool waters and walked towards the Shivling, leaving wet footprints on the stone ghaats. His footprints evaporated quickly over the stone as it cooled from the heat of the day. He was turning his jhanav, a sacred thread that identified his lineage as a Brahmin, as he mumbled his evening prayers under his breath. He tried not to get distracted by the two strangers. His prayers would be interrupted if he acknowledged them. He stopped instead to light a lamp at the Shivling. Once his prayers were done, he momentarily glanced towards the two sitting by the Shivling and gave them a cursory nod, and walked on.

This attention unsettled Shanta and she shifted her weight a little. She covered her neck and forehead—she was not wearing a mangalsutra or kumkum (vermillion), the insignia of a married woman. She imagined the questions in the strangers' mind, and tightened her pull on her saree just a little.

Ratanlal sensed her fears. He looked away wondering how he could pacify her and justify his actions. His eyes rested on two small shallow depressions in the stone near the Shivling. One contained red kumkum. The other held a yellowish powder—turmeric. Kumkum symbolized sanctity and strength, it celebrated life. Married women wore kumkum on their forehead as they were the bearers of life, the strength of a home. Turmeric symbolized purification, cleansing and health. Together, they carried the prayers from the hands of the devotee to the feet of the deity. Laced with religious significance, these two powders lay innocuously side by side, blended by hasty devotion of believers. The powders were somewhat caked from the frequent wet fingers of devotees. But what had dried, had spilled from its cavity into the other. Each powder was two shades of one: one more red than yellow and the other more yellow than red. Not unlike them, Ratanlal and Shanta were here because of their choices. They knew that whatever the outcome of their adventures, their actions would surely affect the other. The sight of these two powders, the kumkum and turmeric powders at that specific moment, only amounted to fate.

A single thought raced through Ratanlal's mind. It would only take a small pinch, a token, to change everything between them. It would let Shanta know he was an honorable man, and still offer her a choice. The day was not over yet.

Ratanlal reached over and gathered a little bit of each powder and turned to Shanta, raising his hand towards her forehead. His gesture silently asked if she wanted this, to be married. She bowed her head in acceptance. Ratanlal leaned in and christened her bare forehead with a pinch of the powders, dusting her moon-like face with the sanctity of the turmeric and kumkum, bathing it in the serenity of a simple but significant ritual. He was marrying her. His actions quelled the doubts in her mind as well as his own. He was honoring her presence in his life as his wife and not as his conquest. As much as he offered her a choice, he had also wanted her to stay. As their eyes met, Ratanlal's captivating smile melted Shanta's heart all over again. He was a good man, she should never have doubted him. As the evening sun melted into the sinuous waves of Narmada, Shanta's fears were erased, she was a married woman, she was content.

In the still and blissful moments that followed, the new couple realized that they had ignored their hunger pangs all day. Ratanlal rushed out to find a fruit vendor near the temple gates just as he was closing shop for the evening. He returned carrying back a few overripe bananas, a cracked coconut and some sitaphal, typical of offerings one would make at a temple, along with a few betel leaves and fixings to make himself a paan, or three, for the long night ahead. Ratanlal found the sitaphal too cumbersome. He pulled out a small dagger from his cumberband and tried to whittle away pieces of tender coconut flesh. Shanta settled on the sitaphal, squeezing the fruit gently to crack it open. She scooped out the fleshy, seeded segments with her thumb, collecting the seeds one by one in the palm of her hand. The few morsels of fruit quelled Shanta's hunger just long enough so she could fall sleep. It had broken her food-fast for the day. It was time to get some rest.

The large bindles made for uncomfortable pillows, yet Shanta rested her head on one of them and tried to sleep while Ratanlal watched over them through the night. While she rested, he assembled a paan for himself. He wiped down the betel leaves carefully, applied a thin layer of chalk-lime to it, and tucked in trimmed pieces of supari and tobacco before creating a small triangular pouch of the leaf and tucking it into his cheek. It would keep him awake. He did not see anyone come to the ghaats at night. Their first night after a symbolic wedding was on the ghaats of the Narmada River. The stone kept them warm. The songs of holy river calmed their fears. The dew of the night cooled their spirits. Nothing could have blessed their marriage more.

Pre-dawn over the waters of Narmada lit up the sky. Ratanlal tapped Shanta's shoulder lightly to awaken her—it was time. He walked over to fetch his horse. She completed her toilette while dawn was still at bay, Ratanlal returned and took his horse to the river for a drink, they had a long day ahead of them. He brought the beast back to the ghaats and handed the reigns to Shanta, undressed to his dhoti, and headed to the river for a bath. His clothes lay in a short pile next to the bindles, and on it, Ratanlal placed the small dagger and a pouch from his cummerbund. He asked her to guard their belongings. He was a man of prayer and ritual and took this opportunity to leisurely bathe in the holy Narmada River, humming a sacred verse to wash away any sins, to help him embark on a new journey of his life with his bride.

"Gange che Yamune chaiva Godavari Saraswati |

Narmade Sindhu Kaveri jalesmin sannidhim kuru | | "

"In this water, I invoke the presence of holy waters from the rivers Ganga, Yamuna, Godavari, Saraswati, Narmada, Sindhu and Kaveri, may these bless and purify my body."

The sounds of his humming faded, leaving Shanta with the melodious notes of his voice in her ear. The sun had only begun to peek over the waters, refreshed from the night's slumber. Shanta's gaze alternated between the glowing horizon, the swirling light and shadows in the currents of the Narmada and the silhouette of her husband amidst it all, rising and falling into the waters as he completed his prayers. There were only a few devotees at the river this morning, and most were headed into the river just like Ratanlal. This was the start of her new life.

What would she address him as, now that he was her husband? Where would they make their home? So many questions and possibilities. She caught herself smiling coyly, and shook her head to break away from those thoughts. They would plan it together; she was going to be the best wife a man could ask for.

Although she was tasked with guarding their things, the spellbinding visual of her husband, and thoughts of her new life kept her distracted. But the sight of two travellers spending the night at the ghaats had not gone unnoticed. While Shanta watched Ratanlal, two men snuck up on her. They grabbed the two large bindles. The clanging of the utensils in one of them startled Shanta. She turned around and shrieked at the sight of the thieves. They reached for the pouch and the dagger but

Shanta grabbed it before they could get that too. She began screaming in fear, waving the dagger at them, clutching the one little pouch that had escaped their looting. She hurried to stand, rushing towards them, hoping they would drop the bindles. But they simply were not intimidated by this petite woman. They began to run away.

Sadly, Ratanlal heard nothing over the gurgling Narmada. There was no one else at the ghaats at that time to help her. Accepting that her attempts to stop the thieves would be futile, Shanta grabbed what remained of their belongings and ran towards the river. She waved her arms at Ratanlal, trying to attract his attention, but his back was turned, his palms join above his head, engrossed in prayer.

Shanta started to call but was confused—how was she to address him? A married woman never addressed her husband by his name. The only time she had spoken to him, she had called him 'Rao', customary for a stranger.

Ignoring the fear of any stray public opinion, she screamed in Marathi:

"Listen! Listen! Can you hear (me) ... thieves, thieves are here...."

Sadly, he heard nothing. She rushed down the steps to get closer, but he was several feet away, facing the rising sun, her soft voice unable to carry over the sounds of the river. By the time she could attract his attention, the thieves were long gone.

Ratanlal rushed to the spot where he had left his bindles. The cold ground only mocked him. He could do nothing. Reporting the theft would mean they would be discovered. Some of the devotees saw this unfold but they were not sure how to help the two strangers. Ratanlal stood silently, dripping from the river waters, letting the realisation of his loss sink in. Shanta crumpled to the ground and sobbed, cursing herself for being distracted, she had failed in her very first wifely duty. Ratanlal sat down on his haunches next to her, holding his head in his hands, unconsciously rocking himself wondering what he would do next.

The only saving grace was that he still had the little pouch from his cummerbund, his wife, and a horse.

Ratanlal and Shanta rode for many days, stopping along the way to find food, resting at a temple here or a shelter there, or sometimes at the base of a tree. At first, Ratanlal had considered stopping in Pune, but it did not seem safe enough. If they rode without stopping, it would take two weeks to get to Goa, a small fishing community along the edge of the western coast of India. The ocean air might do them good, Ratanlal thought. They rode through Nashik, Pune and were headed to Kolhapur, in search of a place far enough away from their old lives, so they could begin their married life without the shackles of fear or judgement.

Shanta had not once asked when they would stop and settle, but they were both a little restless and tired, wanting to find a place to start their lives. Each night they had stopped at a new temple, they sought the refuge of divine powers, hoping the blessing would carry them safely along until they found a place to stop for good.

Once past Pune, they rode through fields of jowar, bajra, ragi, spicy green chillies, sweet sugarcane, and peanuts. Some crops were about ready for the harvest—it was September. This was a fertile land, unlike the dry lands of Indore. The winds felt cooler and there were many mountains around them covered in lush green following the monsoons. And at the foothills of those mountains were fields carpeted with bountiful crops. The tall fields gave them respite from the curious glances of strangers—Shanta was a little excited this far away from home, to be a rebel. Whenever they would stop, she would wander into the fields and return with a fistful of the farmer's crop. A missing sugarcane stick here or there would be alright she thought and at one stop she asked Ratanlal for stick or two so she could enjoy its sweet juices.

Ratanlal was enjoying learning about his bride, the once shy girl was blossoming into a little renegade, and she was a good match to his feisty nature indeed. He chuckled and headed into the fields, his feet sinking in the porous soft soil. But sugarcane proved to be a difficult one to simply break away, it was much harder. The sound of Shanta's giggles challenged Ratanlal and he even tried the tender stalks without any luck—he was annoyed. On his fourth try, he decided to yank the sugarcane stalk out from the soil, roots and all. While he held up his conquest in pride, shaking the stem at her, the mud clods disintegrated, showering him in black dust, Shanta giggled some more. Eager to get to her sugarcane, Shanta ran towards him. But when she got closer, she noticed his furrowed brow and a pained expression.

Ratanlal's palms were stinging—the prickly sugarcane burrs covering his callused hands. The sight of his palm embarrassed and horrified Shanta. His palms were warm and firm, she had never explicitly held his hands in her own before, they were rough and scaled from days of riding. Their eyes met again, and she lowered her gaze to his palm once more, urging him to sit down under a nearby tree. One by one, she plucked the burrs off his palm. Gazing into his palms to pluck each burr was awkward for Shanta, she was holding his hands in her own for the first time. She was overcome—he was her husband but holding hands in broad daylight was impossibly scandalous. She looked around, they were alone in the fields, she resumed plucking the burrs.

Despite the discomfort, Ratanlal was tickled pink and chuckling while his bride's fingers trembled as she became increasingly self-consciousness. Finally, she exclaimed:

"Go away, Rao."

She shoved his palm away from her and turned away, exasperated that he found humour in her hapless plight. Ratanlal let out a hearty laugh and finished the task himself, muttered aloud:

"This is not a suitable task for you, rani-saheb (madam-queen)."

He had addressed her for the first time, with a respectful yet endearing term. She turned her gaze away sighing with blissful content. Sitting at the edge of a field on the cool black soil, with no home to call their own, they had found each other. They rested for a short while and once refreshed, rode towards Kolhapur for the night leaving a single uprooted and half-chewed sugarcane stalk at the edge of the field. The thieves did not want much, thought the farmer as he went about his day the next morning.

Ratanlal's little pouch had held a few gems, and Kolhapur turned out to be a place where they fetched more money than Nashik. The men and women in this little town dressed well and wore flashy ornaments. The money from selling small gems had kept them fed and warm for the past few weeks but this nomadic life could not last for long. Kolhapur was warm and friendly. Its people believed they were blessed by the auspicious Devi Amba-bai Temple, the patron goddess of the region. This was a small but bustling town thriving with business, much like Indore. The marketplace was abuzz even after dusk as people scurried around to get home after the evening aarti (prayers) at the temple.

Ratanlal and Shanta decided to sleep in the shadow of the temple complex, near the doorway for the night; Shanta wanted to receive her first blessings from this mighty and powerful Devi only after she was bathed the following morning. Seeing two weary travellers, and a young couple at that, a flower vendor, Bapu, offered them room and board for the night in exchange for a few annas. Housing weary devotees was a good source of extra income for him, and without a doubt, and he would further entice them with his wares the next morning as they headed for the temple. This was a welcome alternative for both Shanta and Ratanlal. Shanta was thrilled at the prospect of sleeping indoors for one night, with a respectable roof over her head and the privacy of a bathing area for her toilette the next morning.

Their hostess, Vani, was not much older than Shanta. She offered them what she had made for themselves that night—a serving of misal and bhakri, it was a simple fare. Kolhapur was known for its fiery meat dishes, but not in a guest house without notice. Ratanlal and Shanta had arrived quite late and were simply grateful to have a warm nourishing meal after many days on the run.

Bapu and Ratanlal settled to eat their dinner before the women. Ratanlal liked the spice and though he was craving a meat preparation, it would be an inconvenient request at such a late hour. The misal was a stew of matki (Turkish beans or moth beans), cooked down with onions and spices. They could taste the heat of the black pepper, the nuttiness of dried coconut and the unmistakable dagad-phool, a lichen popular in this region. The lichen gave the stew a meaty aroma. A pot of well-made misal stewing in a kitchen sent out invisible messengers, its aromas inviting strangers and friends alike as it floated out into the streets; it made even the most satiated diner hungry. Their hosts' kitchen now smelt like a warm comforting blanket as even its walls were saturated with the aroma of her spices. Ratanlal cleaned his plate in no time, sopping up the misal with large pieces of bhakri. He was famished.

Shanta and Vani ate next. Each morsel was richly flavorful and hugged Shanta's insides. But the spice built up and was too much for Shanta, she was not used to the raw and sharp taste of the Kolhapuri thikhat (cayenne pepper), it began to burn her mouth. Vani and Bapu, were humoured when Shanta asked for more and more water to wash down the spice, but nothing helped. Shanta finally gave up and Vani offered her a serving of taak (buttermilk) and a small portion of jaggery. The jaggery was sweet and the warmth of her mouth melted it into a creamy sweet caramel that soothed the heat from the misal. She was grateful for her hostess.

Shanta helped Vani clean up as the men sat on the stoop and chatted over some tobacco laden paan. The household quieted for the night. Vani slept near the kitchen, while Bapu slept on the stoop for the night. Shanta and Ratanlal slept on two simple mattresses in the main room near the kitchen, this was their first bed in many days.

Loud temple bells rang through Kolhapur at pre-dawn. Temple priests believed these woke the deity from her restful slumber along with her devotees. This was the town of Amba-bai, or Maha-Shanta or Devi Ambabai, a deity known by many names. The temple itself was a stunning sight to behold, with a grand carved arched main entrance to the east and a group of several tall lamp towers, all carved in black volcanic stone welcoming the faithful. The doorways still had some of the fading garlands from earlier celebrations. Priests of different ages were milling in and out of the temple, rushing bare feet through the inner courtyard, carrying platters of flowers, prayer books, or jars of water. The flower sellers were hovering around the eager morning devotees touting baskets laden with blue lotus blossoms. It was going to be time for the morning darshan (viewing) soon.

Ratanlal paid Bapu handsomely as they got ready to leave. And yet, Vani felt like something was missing. She sensed that there was something naïve about Shanta who appeared too young to be married, was not wearing a mangalsutra and yet had kumkum on her forehead. Shanta was not dressed well enough for the first darshan, her saree appeared as though it had endured much wear and tear over their long journey.

Vani knew what she had to do. She found a new nav-wari and a dozen green bangles with flecks of gold and offered it to Shanta:

"Think of me as your tai (sister). A beautiful young girl as you should be suitably dressed for her first blessing at the temple of the benevolent Goddess Ambabai."

As Vani urgingly thrust her gifts into her hand, Shanta's eyes teared up, she was moved at this sisterly gesture. These were not expensive gifts but fitting for a newly married woman. Vani placed a pinch of kumkum and turmeric on Shanta's forehead, symbolically accepting her into the sisterhood of married women. Shanta returned the honor, by placing the two sacred powders on Vani's forehead but had no gifts to give her in exchange. Instead, she touched her hostess' feet out of respect, as she would a family elder. As Vani placed two warm palms on Shanta's head to bless her, Shanta tried to control her flood of emotions. She had not expected to find such sisterly kindness in a stranger's home.

Shanta hurriedly adorned her new saree and bangles, heartened by the gift of acceptance and affection from her hostess. As they left, Vani took a small piece of kohl from her eyes and placed a black mark on Shanta's cheek, to keep away the evil eye, she said. Shanta was brimming with gratitude at these simple acts of warmth and acceptance. She emerged from the guest house, her face glowing with happiness, ready to head to the temple with her husband, Ratanlal.

The crisp creases on Shanta's new saree, her clinking green glass bangles and her coy smiles beckoned a gesture of appreciation from her husband. A vendor carrying a basket of fragrant jasmines approached them. Ratanlal purchased a foot-long threaded gajara (garland) for Shanta's hair. She was his wife and there would be time for more adornments—this would do for now.

As Shanta attached it to her bun, her hand unconsciously stroked her bare neck—she was missing a mangalsutra, the symbolic necklace that would identify her as a married woman. Ratanlal saw it from the corner of his eye and walked to another vendor selling threads of black and fake gold beads, he merely chose one for her, paid for it and proceeded to the temple. There would be a better time and place to purchase a suitable piece of jewellery for his wife. Their host had sold them a platter of blue lotuses and coconut offerings for the deity. They were all set to seek the blessings of this mighty and powerful goddess.

Ratanlal and Shanta crossed the threshold of the temple, bowing down to touch the stone like countless others had done before. Stepping into the temple complex slowly felt like a renewal of faith—they walked, guided by the many others there. They were all moving towards the inner sanctum, waiting to seek the blessings of the devi. Jostled and pushed around, they made their way in.

As she approached the inner sanctum, Shanta was struck by the beauty of the small idol, no larger than a young child. The Devi was carved in black stone, dressed in a green saree, adorned with gold jewellery, and surrounded by bushels of flowers. Her eyes were carved of a white marble, an awe-inspiring sight. Her head held a large golden crown with a bold vermillion mark, her forehead was covered in yellow turmeric, she wore a large beaded nose-ring. Devi Ambabai was striking, mesmerising.

With her head covered, Shanta had walked in with folded palms, while Ratanlal had carried in the platter of offerings to the priest. The priest was chanting hymns and prayers in Sanskrit. He took offerings without breaking his own rhythm, cracked open the coconut and placed one-half back in their platter.

He then returned to what he was doing.

Swaying the glowing lamp, the aarti, the priest waved the camphor and ghee flames to appease the benovelent Goddess. He sang her praises, asked for blessings, all the while orchestrating a dance of the flames. A magnetic cadence of ancient Sanskrit poetry flowed effortlessly from his lips like curls of smoke rising from a slowly burning fire. When he stopped to breathe, he turned towards the devotees, holding out the aarti as they reached over to receive their blessings. Shanta and Ratanlal cupped their hands over the flame and bowed down, they were blessed.

There was a momentary lull in the throng of devotees, and the priest asked if there were any special prayer requests. Ratanlal fished out the inexpensive mangalsutra and without a word exchanged, the priest understood. He began chanting more blessings on behalf of the couple as Ratanlal held up the simple threads and proceeded to tie them around Shanta's neck. This was more proper, he thought, and Shanta could not contain her emotions, her eyes began to well up with tears. The priest finally handed Shanta an additional token blessing, a veni (braided garland) from the flowers that had just moments ago adorned the deity.

Shanta wondered about that moment. Those dark stone temple walls had heard so many prayers and pleas before, and the goddess has blessed so many before her. She was merely one among the many here. But why was she different? And why did she feel different? Perhaps because her marriage was now recognised? As several other priests had done in the short time they were married, this priest too had blessed them too but being more ceremoniously married, however simply, at the grandiose Kolhapur Devi Ambabai's temple seemed to centre them both. Their commitment to each other was now cemented. Perhaps this blessing would usher their good fortune, they would find a place to make their home.

Ratanlal and Shanta rode over the next few days down towards the coast of Goa. They saw more fields, farmers, streams and waterfalls along the way. In the distance, the ocean became visible and made them restless even more. Sawantwadi was on the way, it would make a good place to stop for the night. Sawantwadi had been the seat of the Bhonsale kings for a long time; there was a simple palace with an arched wooden door and windows that looked out under awnings into the lush palms. There was a lake in that village with shops all around for trinkets and household sundries. There was something familiar about being back in village with some princely ties.

But when they got there, all Shanta wanted to do was continue on. The air had changed, it seemed saltier, different. There was a certain crispness to the mountain air of Sawantwadi, the people spoke a slightly different kind of Marathi, but she simply wanted to find a place to settle down, to be able to bathe and cook at her own will, to be married. She ached to be at peace with all their choices. After a night in another guest house in Sawantwadi, like the one in Kolhapur, Ratanlal and Shanta rode towards Panjim. Goa seemed farther away and Shanta's restlessness was showing. They needed to settle down.

The cashew and jackfruit groves of the coast were fragrant and heady, perhaps they might enjoy living here. Panjim was a tiny village of fishermen and farmers, some Hindu, some Catholics, all distinctly Goan. They spoke a strange dialect of Marathi, Konkani; the language combined snippets of Portuguese words. They were generally kind and friendly but a little suspicious of two young people who came on a horse—horses were not common here. They found temporary respite as paying guests in a cashew farmer's home, but Ratanlal decided that he would have to find a place to rent for a little longer. In a few days, Ratanlal had found a small house to rent, had sold his horse to the landlord and purchased their first set of utensils to begin their simple married life.

But Panjim held its own challenges. Unlike Indore or Kolhapur, Panjim was a place of frugality. The villagers lived from season to season, some were rice or cashew farmers, others fishermen, teachers, priests, coconut vendors, Portuguese soldiers, and government officers. The women did not have the desire to get jewellery advice from a stranger; instead, they lusted after carefully tinkered jewellery crafted by people who spoke to them in their own tongue. Shanta tried to understand how to cook here, not familiar with the coconut based fish curries or pungent meat preparations. She learnt how to make a few things from a kindly old woman who lived a few houses down from them; a fish stew in coconut milk and a spicy shrimp dish—but the rice grains were short and lumpy when cooked. She enjoyed the local bread and it became a convenient addition to their meals. Ratanlal quickly learnt that people spent their meagre earnings on a kind of cheap local favorite, a liquor call Feni. Ratanlal was used to British whisky. He simply could not bear to go near that stuff.

Accustomed to the dry interior countryside, the wet coastal weather was difficult on both of them. Shanta tried very hard to get over the humidity and overwhelming salty ocean breeze but it seemed to cling to everything and everyone. She asked Ratanlal to take her to a place where there was a mountain or a river or a temple where she could pray; she just needed the space to breathe easy. There was a little temple, the Shanta-durga temple nearby, perched on a tiny hillock, surrounded by mango orchards. It was peaceful. The Mandovi River was nearby, but it was wide,

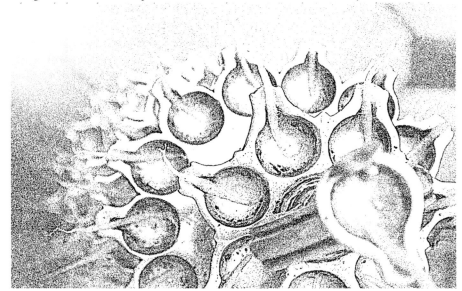

angry. She missed the spontaneous splendour of rivers she had imagined and seen before, even the Narmada's as they sat by it that first night. In comparison, Mandovi's waters were muddy and unpredictable, lethargic.

There were many temples and churches around, but they represented what she missed, her home, her mother and her people, more than she would admit. She had chosen to elope with Ratanlal; there was no going back to her past. Her shy and reserved nature returned. When the people around spoke Konkani it sounded like gibberish to her simple ears. She imagined them gossiping and snickering at her. Everything unsettled her—the language, culture, the people and the fishy foods. The smells of the market were too much for her, so Ratanlal would bring home vegetables and groceries that he liked. But a skilled jeweller did not make for a skilled shopper and Shanta's kitchen and her own health suffered. She remained increasingly homebound, lest people asked questions that she did not understand or have all the answers for.

The walls of their little two-room house felt like they were closing in on her, Ratanlal was gone most of the day in search of work; the heavy, salty ocean air made her queasy, she had lost her appetite. She was pregnant, and that added to her discomfort. Although Ratanlal was thrilled, he saw no joy in Shanta's eyes as she shared her news. She missed her mother even more now, and they had not befriended enough people in the village who might help take care of her. There was no one to observe the pregnancy rituals or prepare nutritious meals. Shanta began to shrink under the weight of her impending and lonely motherhood. While Ratanlal tried his best, the pregnancy continued to become a depressing sheath. Shanta hated herself for feeling so alone. Somewhere past the sugarcane fields and the misty mountains, the musky humid and clammy air of Panjim had stolen her spunk. They would have to find a new home soon. This adventure was no longer exciting. A ferry capsized in the Mandovi River one evening, and Shanta's fears got the better of her. Mani, their daughter arrived the next morning, a few weeks early. Shanta was weak with exhaustion, Ratanlal feared for her health. For everyone's sake, Ratanlal had to find a new town where he could find work and they could continue to live in the true essence of the word.

Two weary passengers and a month-old Mani headed off to a new city. They were going to start their lives over, and raise their family in the big city of Mumbai.

CHAPTER FOUR

To The Post Office

Thakor knew nothing of what his Ba was facing back in Lanva, of her arrest, her release or the debt that hovered over her soul. No one wrote to him. The weight of abandoning her was great on Thakor; it gnawed at him each day. When he reached Mumbai, he had less than a rupee in his pocket. He could buy a few meals but there was no place to sleep. He finally befriended a local newspaper seller, who in exchange for helping unload the newspapers, gave him a roof over his head each night.

Thakor spent hours each day walking through the wholesale markets of Mumbai, discovering all kinds of new places—rows upon rows of shops dedicated to grains or precious metal, lanes with jewellers trading in pearls, diamonds, gold, cloth merchants and more. These were the markets of Jhaveri Bajar, Dana Bajar and Nul Bajar where volume and wholesale merchants mingled and small vendors found a way to make some quick money. This was a different world for a boy who had until now lived in and around the hot arid fields of Gujarat, visited communal fairs for fun, and seen only turbaned merchants for much of his life.

After many days of searching, Thakor finally found work in the kitchen of a local Company cafeteria in Byculla as their busboy. The pay was meagre but he could eat whatever he wanted. His smiles were precious and he was always intrigued by food, encouraging people to eat more. Within a year, he had a spot inside the kitchen, chopping vegetables. He could do anything, but would not work with meat, after all he was a Hindu, a vegetarian at that. This city could have his sweat and blood, but would not soil his religion.

Time passed briskly as Thakor spent most of his days working in the cafeteria or exploring the new city he now called home. The newspaper seller allowed him to stay in the shop at night for a small rent. He could read the papers and keep up with the world—he would find a way to become successful. Having been a farmer's son, he had lived a life of essentials, not the excesses that this city doled out. Although initially overwhelmed with the adjustments, confidence quickly returned to Thakor, that something would come about of his adventures in this great city. There simply had to be more.

At work, Thakor would often accompany the cafeteria kitchen staff to the market each morning, charming his way into the hearts of the vendors to secure the best produce before the crack of dawn. He would spend the afternoons helping make confections for the cafeteria for the next day. His goal was to earn enough to send at least ten rupees to Johari-ba each month, from his salary of twenty rupees. But his job was difficult; ten rupees was impossible when he earned only five to start with! When his pay finally rose to ten rupees, nearly two years after he had left Lanva, Thakor sent half of it to Johari-ba. With each passing day, Thakor's treats became legendary. He was skillfully combining his hankering for the taste of traditional Rajasthani desserts with the desire to share his love of food with the diners. After working from the crack of dawn to when the last plate was cleared from the cafeteria, Thakor finally won over the proprietor with his hard work and charm. Four years after he started, he was promoted to head confectioner; a prestigious position for a boy who had started with only a handful of cooking skills. He celebrated by making a batch of gulab jamuns out of gharari mava (milk solids from camel's milk), deep fried treats, soaked in a decadent sugar syrup. There were only a few places to buy gharari mava, it gave his gulab jamuns an unmistakable edge over the others in the market. Every time he made them, he was reminded of the headstrong runaway that he was. He came from a small village on the edge of the desert who had emerged from the rigours of city life, soaked in the sweetness of the rewards of hard work. Some part of him would always belong to the tall fields of bajra and jowar, and to the dusty desert at the edge of Rajasthan.

The new-found confidence gave Thakor the ability to imagine, to dabble in the workings of a cafeteria, recognising that his passion was to make people happy, with delicious food—but the confidence did not last for long. Another two years went by and he continued to garner a greater command of his skills but it also made him restless. Thakor needed more than skill to run a restaurant of his own, he needed money and lots of it. As much as people loved his food, they did not have enough to give him a large loan.

Today was the first of the month, March 1928. Thakor looked at the paper notes he had received as pay. He knew that within a few hours, he would hold only half of it in his palms as he handed the rest to the man at the post office. They would arrange a money order to Lanva, and send ten rupees into the ageing hands of his Ba. Perhaps the hungry palms of his unemployed brother might intercept the money order and postcard. Suraj had always been the baby of the house, perhaps he was still asking his mother for money. In the nearly ten years after he left Lanva, no one from his village or even his family had made an attempt to come visit him. He had always included the address of his landlord, but no one wrote back. That afternoon, Thakor made another large batch of gulab jamuns. He saved up a dozen soaked pieces for the proprietor's wife and left them next to the cash register with a simple note; as of that afternoon, he had quit.

With his last pay in hand, Thakor headed in the direction of the post office. But his feet dragged, what was he going to do next? What would his mother say? The March skies were hot and he spotted a tea seller down the road from the post office. The sight reminded Thakor of the train station stop in Amdavad. He had come far, but how far did he need to still go? Tea had brought him a little clarity once before, why not take a sip, he thought to himself. Perhaps he could explain to Suraj and Johari-Ba, so they knew not to expect another money order for a while? What if they did not understand?

Thakor found some change to pay the tea vendor, took his tumbler and looked around for a place to sit. An adjacent stoop looked clean and dry and he absentmindedly sat down. The shadow of the awning comforted him as he sipped the hot brew and fell into deep thought. The tiny steel tumbler held perhaps a half cup of a strong caffeinated brew; a light frothy white top covered an oak coloured liquid, made with tea dust, sugar, and diluted milk. A strong aroma of dried ginger and lemon grass leaves in the tea masked it's over-brewed bitterness. Thakor unconsciously compared it to the rich milk from their water buffaloes in Lanva. The thought of gentle water buffaloes comforted him. His cha in Lanva would smell of them, of the hay and cud of the animal shed. This city cha from the vendor was weak, cheap and almost tawdry in comparison. It made him homesick but his preoccupation kept him coming back, reaching for a small sip each time.

"What is it, mister? Your thoughts run deep."

A deep, slightly raspy voice broke Thakor out of his melancholic gaze. The voice spoke in Marathi, the common dialect of this busy city. Thakor was still getting familiar with the local language—somewhere between disembarking from the puffing train at Victoria Terminus and Byculla, and over the many years since he arrived he had almost forgotten his mother tongue. He turned around to see a pair of grey-green eyes staring at him from under a large white cotton turban. His own blank stare into the afternoon sunlit by lanes had momentarily blinded him. Thakor blinked a few times before he was able to see who spoke to him. The voice belonged to a handsome man in his late thirties perhaps; it floated from underneath moustached lips stained with tobacco, paan leaves and the lingering of cigar smoke. The man was sitting on the floor on a low mattress in the cool shade of a large workspace, his back resting in a well-worn bolster and his fingers playing with a quill over a large ledger. A short little secretary desk, meant for the floor was on the mattress to his side. A single boogadi (earring) on the top of his left earlobe caught Thakor's eye, as the red and green glass beads added a tinge of colour in this ivory-cotton space. The man wore a pair of ruby studs—Thakor liked men who wore jewellery, just like the men did in Lanva.

Not knowing what else to say, Thakor replied in Marathi:

"I hope you don't mind my sitting here."

The man responded in a slightly humorous tone:

"If my stoop gives you relief, it has given me some good karma. And if anything, I know that one can never have too much good karma. I know how it feels, if you like, you can sit inside with me. It is my tea time too, the floors of my office are a little cooler and the seating is a little more comfortable."

He tinkled a little hand-bell. A young boy of about ten emerged and was instructed to get some cold water for the stranger.

Thakor smiled and took off his large leather sandals at the stoop, wondering why this man seemed so kindly. He dusted his feet unconsciously as he took his little tumbler with him and came in. He had not been invited into an office like this before—the room was dark and cool and a little hand-held fan beckoned for attention, hanging precariously off the little secretary desk. The awkward silence lasted until the boy returned with water and a dry towel in case the guest wanted to freshen up. The boy asked in a hushed voice:

"Bai-saheb (madam) has asked if anything else is to be sent out for Rao-sahib and his guest."

Thakor's host instructed the boy:

"Hmm, bai-saheb is very perceptive. It looks like my new friend and I can use something to eat. Would she be able to toss up a fresh chiwda, perhaps? And if we can have some, two fresh cups of cha—with a splash of cream. Oh, yes! Return that tumbler to that no good cha-wala outside—flavoured mud water, that terrible thing he calls cha!"

The older man turned to Thakor and smiled. Instructions had been given, they could now chat in peace. Thakor had walked this way, up and down the street countless times, never once needing to understand who was here or what happened behind the stone stoops and underneath wooden awnings of the little shops. He came in before dawn and left well into the night, and each time, none of the doors were open. Today, he was sitting with a stranger in one of those establishments, whose stone floor was so much cooler than the hot pavement outside or the stoops, waiting for a fresh cup of cha. Thakor took the cold water and walked back to the stoop, splashing some on his face and on his feet to cool them off, rinsing his mouth of the flavours of the tea stall cha. He saved the towel and took out his own small muslin handkerchief, dabbing his forehead and cheeks, feeling refreshed.

Setting down the lota (spherical container) of water by the door, Thakor stepped back in. He was unsure how he would repay this stranger for the kindness and if he would make it in time to the post office before it closed. The cha came first in two small ceramic cups, unlike the stained tea tumbler from the tea stall. A few minutes later, the boy brought down two small bowls of chiwda and the two men sat in silence enjoying it.

The chiwda was simple, made of puffed rice and small crunchy little kernels of tangy and spicy nuts and curry leaves—the light snack was warm and tasty. The cha tasted so much better than the one from the tea stall. It was neither spiced nor had any foam on top, it was rich and milky. There was a light film of cream, suggesting that the milk had been poured into the tea after the black brew was served in the cup. Thakor had missed fresh cream. He looked up and saw bits of cream hanging off his host's moustache, he tried not to snicker. The man resembled a cat that was about to lick his whiskers, instead, he used his forefinger to flick off the cream and smoothed his moustache. He said:

"Rao, people rarely come to visit me without a reason, so it is nice to share a cup of cha with a young chap like you. It has been a long while since I chatted with a new friend. For no reason, I am enjoying your company very much."

Thakor only smiled, he was happy to have met this stranger. He was a man of few words and wondered if his anxiety was showing as the silence became awkward. His host waited patiently for his new friend to confide in him. Finally, Thakor broke the silence with an informal but respectful salutation:

"Kaka (uncle), thank you so much for your kindness. I am Thakor, and I used to work at the Company cafeteria. Not anymore though, I quit today. I have a lot on my mind; I must go to the post office before it closes and send a money order today to my Ba. Perhaps you will allow me the honour of returning another time when I have some joyous news? I can bring you a dabba (tin) of my finest gulab jamuns if I am able to resolve my current problem quickly."

He was lying optimistically for he had no clue where he would be the next day. The man smiled and nodded in agreement. He affirmed his faith in the future with an encouraging note.

"Aha, you are the Company cook! I have heard about you and your gulab jamuns! I never turn away a new friend, especially one who can bring me a special batch of gulab jamuns! Bai-saheb would love a special treat like that too. But gulab jamuns or not, do stop by, even if it is to read the newspaper. You are welcome anytime. If nothing else, we can see how I can lighten your load. I have been doing business with people in this town long enough."

Thakor looked into the man's eyes. They were smiling back at him, light wrinkles forming near the corners—he was warm and kindhearted and Thakor hoped he would have a reason to visit him again soon and repay his kindness. With folded palms, he bowed to bid this man goodbye:

"Salutations, Kaka, I shall return soon."

Thakor found his worn leather sandals right where he had left them. Above it was a small wooden sign he had not noticed before, with the words "Shri Ratanlal Jadhav" painted on it. There was no reference to the services he provided. Thakor was intrigued by his generous and charismatic new friend, Ratanlal Kaka. He headed to the post office only to find it had closed just a few minutes before.

And while Thakor walked away towards the post office, a young girl of perhaps seven or eight skipped into the room and sat down by Ratanlal's ledger, curiously flipping the pages, and asked:

"Baba (father), who was that man?"

Ratanlal replied gazing out into the street:

"A new friend, my dearest Mani. He makes the best gulab jamuns I am told and he has offered to bring some the next time he visits, especially for you and your mother."

Little Mani's eyes lit up, she had a sweet tooth. Gulab jamuns sounded splendid.

Thakor returned to the post office the next day hoping his postcard would explain that this would be his last money order for a while. He had no idea what was in store for him.

CHAPTER FIVE

Of Woodfires & Bonfires

1915-1925, ALIBAG & MUMBAI, MAHARASHTRA

Alibag was a coastal village of fisher folk and farmers, a region whose people toiled in the fields a few of months of the year and engaged in odd jobs through the rest. It held the local collectorate, courts district offices, and governmental buildings for the area—tucked between the raging and unpredictable Arabian Sea to the west and the foothills of the Western Ghats to the east. Plenty of fishing villages dotted the coastline, up and down from Alibag, with paddy fields and creeks that connected one parcel of land to another. And amidst all of this, was Elphinstone High School, with a small student body of young men and a handful of young women who all came here to study in English, especially if they could afford it.

Among them were Damodar and his older brother Shantaram, sons of the village priest Ganpatrao Vaidya. While some of their classmates came from nearby villages, these boys lived in Alibag. Being Brahmin boys, they were also lucky for their father wanted them to study. They were a family of priests. Their father owned half a village worth of paddy fields. But the boys must be well versed in the ways of the world as well, the patriarch insisted. So off to school they went each day to learn reading, writing, history and basics of arithmetic. Before he headed to their conventional school, Shantaram would spend a few hours at the temple for his first lessons chanting Sanskrit shlokas, learning traditional rituals—all part of his training to become a priest—he was would be the one to carry on the family traditions.

Damodar and Shantaram had one sister, Sumati, the middle child. She was older than Damodar by two years and younger than Shantaram by one. Sumati was not as lucky as she barely learnt to read and write through the age of thirteen. She was betrothed at fifteen, to be married at eighteen. Once she stopped grade school, she was thrust into the fine art of becoming a 'sugrin-gruhini' or the good housewife. Sitting around her aunts and mother, she was taught how to make up six preparations out of the colocasia leaves and the fruits of jackfruit, umpteen kinds of vegetable and fruit preserves and sun-dried treats that could be added to meal times—as any frugal housewife should know. More often it was easier to find her in the kitchen around the small wood-burning stoves or in the back courtyard, fussing with a sun-dried preparation. Although she yearned to read, to study and go to school like her brothers, she was not allowed to. Instead, Damodar and Shantaram would read to her from their books, a poem here and there, or a verse or two, never more. Sometimes they practiced their elocution skills on her as she giggled at their English. Shantaram or Dada (older brother) was good at making her laugh as he imitated his Sanskrit teacher's repetitive instructions about proper enunciations—Damodar, or Damu as she called him, was always intense. Attending religious ceremonies was part of Shantaram's training. So, as good brothers they would take Sumati, or Tai (sister) with them to the evening bhajans at the nearby temples when they could, or to the many small and large religious fairs several times a year. There was not much else to do for three young Brahmin children.

When Shantaram completed high school, his focus shifted back to Sanskrit and religious studies. In a year or so, he would need to be ready to lead the temple prayers. Sumati found it easier to help with Shantaram's studies than conventional learning. She was to be married soon—she had never met her husband, perhaps it was for the best, she thought. What good was it to learn about the worldly matters if her saasar (married home), would be tucked away in another little village a hundred kilometres south of her maher (mother's home)? As someone had teased at her:

"The soul of a woman resides in her husband."

Damodar was a curious young lad, an idealist, and proficient in math, history, and Sanskrit. Unlike his brother, he wanted to be a teacher. The little village of Alibag had been lucky to have the only English medium school in the area, and Damodar wished there would be more. "I will have my own school one day," he had promised himself.

Although it served many villages around them, most of Damodar's classmates were from Alibag. It was too expensive to take a bus and get to school each day. There were only a few girls in his class, and one was Pearl Isac.

A shy girl, one of the ninety-some Jewish people who also inhabited that sleepy village, Pearl lived just a few steps away from the Magen Aboth Synagogue, one of the only two synagogues within a fifty-kilometer radius of Alibag. This little pink building was tucked away in the back of town, near where the fisher folk lived, across from the rice and poha mills. It served the small local Bene Israel community. Pearl would often walk to school with one of her three brothers: Solomon, Samuel or David. The courtyard walls of their house were tall; they were a private family and Damodar never quite understood how many people lived in that house until later.

Much like the Vaidyas, the Isacs had lived in Alibag for many generations. But unlike the Vaidya's who once lived further south in Ratnagiri, the Isac ancestors had fled Palestine centuries ago to find their own place in India and had settled in in Alibag where it seemed safe—they had room to be their own.

Mr Isac, Pearl's father was a maritime man, often away at sea for months. He had not been lucky—his first wife passed away leaving him with a six-year-old son, Samuel, and his second wife passed away too, leaving him with a four-year-old daughter, Pearl. With two young ones on hand, a job that took him away from his children for many months, and no interest in marrying for the third time, Mr. Isac did not have a choice but to entrust them to the care of his sister Beth in the insulated little village of Alibag, where she was raising two boys of her of own: David and Solomon. Perhaps the Isac children would stay connected to their roots in Beth's care.

As a widow herself, Beth welcomed her brother's allowance towards his children's upbringing; it was definitely less expensive to live in a small village than in Mumbai, the big city everyone called Bombay. But when their father was away, Samuel and Pearl never quite figured out how to be real siblings with each other. Aunty Beth would try to keep the peace; the boys somehow got along but Pearl was often the odd one out. Aunty Beth was kind, she taught them prayers, and they would often take a walk to the market together but not much more.

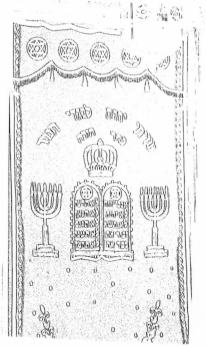

However, Pearl missed her father desperately and would spend much of her time reading, trying to distract herself. The Synagogue would normally have been a good place to meet other young girls like her, but the Bene Israel population of the area was so small, it was not a very active religious community. They ate and lived much like the locals, choosing from fresh fish that their markets offered, and made friends with the Muslim community to sometimes get the best meats. The most she attempted that was special was an occasional malida for a birthday when the flattened rice poha was fresh in the local markets, Sandan (crumbly steamed semolina wedges) for Rosh Hashanah, and perhaps malpua for Hanukkah if she had a spare egg or two in her pantry. Keeping a Kosher kitchen was easy because money was scarce.

Pearl's father wanted better things for his children, particularly his daughter—an education and a career. Sensing Pearl's loneliness, Aunty Beth would teach her what little French she knew, a few times a week. At her Bat Mitzvah, she gifted Pearl a book of French poems. Although Pearl struggled to read it she kept it by her bedside, hoping one day she would understand it all. It had fantastical verses about beautiful things, Aunty Beth said. But for now, she had something else to do; to learn a language nearly no one around her understood so she could escape, even if in spirit, elsewhere.

When grade school progressed into high school, Pearl found herself to be the only girl in a classroom of boys! Damodar was one of her classmates. She often snickered at his fidgety behaviour and always thought his idealism was far too progressive in this little village but she humoured him anyways. His brotherly love for his sister was endearing; she wished she had such a bond with her brothers. Pearl asked to meet Sumati one day but Damodar declined, telling her that she was to be married soon—he would invite her to his Tai's wedding.

The wedding in a Hindu priest's home was not a lavish affair. Sarees were purchased for the bride and a few of the older women on either side of the wedding party, good shawls for the groom and the older men, and Damodar and Shantaram each got a new dhotar (dhoti), a new jhabba (tunic) and a new cap. The boys were excited for their sister but sad that she would live so far away. Their sadness was magnified when just a few days before the Tai's wedding Damodar and Shantaram learned that her husband was a widower with three children to raise! Would she be living in a mud hut in a village half the size of theirs? Damodar was furious—how could his parents burden his sister like that? He was still too young to protest—his opinion did not matter. Sadly, Sumati had been preparing for this new life for a few years and was resigned to her fate. Her parents knew better—she had planned no other life—they were no longer children.

Pearl came to Sumati's wedding. She could not discern that Damodar's sadness was not because she would be far away, but because she would be someone's second wife. When she learnt of it, she empathised with Damodar's pain even more. She was the daughter of her father's second wife. It was not a good way to begin a family.

Disturbed by his parent's decisions, once he finished high school, Damodar headed to Mumbai for college. His Tai was married and dada was immersed in chanting and rituals. This was not a life for him. He would go see what all the 'bonfires' in Mumbai were all about and perhaps make something of himself with a college education. They all called the city 'Bombay,' he should start practising to call it that, thought Damodar or they will know he was a simple village boy. Meanwhile, Pearl chose a girl's hostel in Lonavala, inland and away from the coast—she wanted something different as did her father. It was safer, he insisted. He handed her a small alarm clock from his last trip from Japan; it was a small cube encased in cobalt blue glass, with a tiny key in the back. She cherished it; it would remind her of her father's punctuality. When Damodar and Pearl parted, they promised to write to each other.

It was 1924 when young Damodar arrived in Bombay, a city stirring with patriotic fervour, energised by passionate pleas of satyagrahis (freedom fighters) for independence of body, mind, and spirit—to break away from the tyranny of the British Raj. The idealism of the pre-Independence freedom movement had made an indelible mark on the psyche of the locals. Groups of young men would commune secretly to listen to the speeches of Gandhi over the radio or read banned literature— all with the purpose of coming together to secure freedom for the country. Streets were filled with men every evening—a sea of black caps and jackets over kurtas jostling along in marches and rallies, carrying torches to light the way. Women gathered in other places in peaceful prayer meetings and also to talk about how they could participate in the efforts of their brethren. All ages of people walked the city streets for many hours of the day, holding banners and chanting slogans, hoping to energise, to protest, to be part of something bigger than them—the freeing of a nation.

Large groups of people gathered to burn foreign-made clothes and garments, chanting more slogans, pledging solidarity. Some chanted Gandhi's famous words as they shed their clothes:

"In burning my foreign clothes, I burn my shame."

The 'bonfires' were frequent and often followed by the arrests of those who held them.

The riots were a new kind of Holi, many people were arrested and later released—others were not. News headlines carried word of these protests in local papers and sometimes made news across the world. Yes, the world needed to hear of this small city and its mighty youth. In each letter that he wrote to Pearl, Damodar detailed what he saw; the bloody heads of his friends when they were hurt in the riots, the dark evenings when people gathered in large maidans, of street corners that became markers and meeting points for satyagrahis, the glow of the bonfires he witnessed from up close and from afar and the fire burning in the hearts and minds of the locals.

Pearl read them, but at first had nothing to write back, except to tell him how pleasant the weather was in Lonavala, or how often the mountains were covered in a fog. As she read more in newspapers, she started to ask about the rallies. Were there any women's rallies? How did the women participate in the bonfires? Did he get to attend any of the speeches by that man they called Gandhi? Was it easy to buy clothes that were made with 'khadi?' Did he wear clothes made of 'khadi'? Some of these conversations had to be carefully had for Pearl only suspected that their mail was being read. But Damodar had no idea how the women's rallies were being conducted—he was surrounded only by men. Being in an all-women's hostel was perhaps even more isolating than her father had imagined. And although Damodar's letters did not answer all her questions, in some small measure they kept Pearl connected to the outside world, where things were far more real.

Being away from his home made Damodar homesick. Returning home to Alibag was neither easy nor inexpensive. One would take a ferry from Bhau-cha-dhakka Wharf, over to Dharamtar across the Arabian Sea and then board a bus from Dharamtar to Alibag. The alternative was a very long bus ride that was even more time-consuming—Tai lived even farther away. She could read a little, so he would write her a postcard—she seldom replied. Dada was busy with his training to formally become a priest; he would not have time for idle talk or a visit from his brother. He was happy to have Pearl, the one person to communicate with, who shared his roots, who came from the same place that he did.

Damodar started participating in the freedom struggles, attending rallies and marches. Sometimes, when he was not at college, he would join young men like himself on campaign trails into the villages of Maharashtra. He had heard Gandhi speak once, and was quite taken by his persuasive speech—foreign goods needed to be boycotted, freedom from foreign rule was necessary, and so was frugality. Gandhi had spoken often of his vegetarian habits and Damodar found it easy to adapt to the same principles. He looked forward to joining other youth on the campaign trails.

The satyagrahis were resolved to follow strict Gandhian principles of nonviolence, acceptance, frugality and abstinence from addiction. Their campaign trails were filled with hardships: walking long stretches on dusty roads, through dry and desolate villages in the summer heat wearing simple cotton, handspun clothes, and simple footwear or none at all, eating whatever food that was offered without remorse and keeping the propaganda strong. They met with the poorest of the poor, who unknown to them, had starved themselves to save up food for the young campaigners. Each villager would host eight to ten satyagrahis for the night. Damodar would often prefer to spend the night with a Brahmin household, a vegetarian home, so there would be no meat around to soil his Brahmanical upbringing. And even in the poorest of Brahmin homes, banana leaves or shallow earthen bowls were laid out bearing sustenance—sometimes a varan bhaat or pithla bhaat, perhaps a rice bhakri or if they were lucky, some rice papad—all served straight from blackened pots simmering precariously on a triad of three stones, a configuration that made up their stove. Damodar started each meal the way he was taught as a young Brahmin boy, spreading a little bit of water around his humble meal, and folding his hands to say two prayers:

"Om Saha Naav-Avatu | Saha Nau Bhunaktu | Saha Viiryam Karavaavahai | Tejasvi Naav-Adhiitam-Astu Maa Vidvissaavahai | Om Shaantih Shaantih Shaantih ||"

"Om, may God protect us both. May God nourish us both. May we work together with energy and vigor. May our study be enlightening, and not giving rise to hostility. Om, Peace, Peace, Peace."

And then:

"Vadani kaval gheta naam ghya shri-hariche l Sahaj havan hote naam gheta phukache l Jivan kari jivitva anna he purn-brahma l Udar-bharan nohe janije yadnya-karma ll I ll"

"While taking a mouthful of food, chant the name of God. The food is easily offered as an offering to God when his name is said. The food gives life to us as it is completes God(s) principle. Having food is not just filling the stomach but is a type of fire-sacrifice."

Setting aside a morsel for the spirits, he ate his meals with simple joy. The freshly made warm food was basic, rustic and simple and the aromas heavenly though it had but a few ingredients. It reminded him of home, he was satisfied.

Some evenings they would gather with the other Satyagrahis for a recap of their efforts and to plan the next day; at other times, it was to gather the villagers in a group to share Gandhi's vision of the future for their country.

Damodar's nights on the campaign trail were spent under the open sky on dung-plastered courtyards alongside other young men from the campaign. As morning came, the fog lifted from the courtyard, and the sounds of the morning filled the air—the calls of mynahs and other woodland birds, the tinkling bells of sheep and goats as their herders took them grazing. Their host family would offer them a morning meal before the young men headed off again. Tea and coffee were deemed addictive and therefore unsuitable to a satyagrahi's resolve towards stronger willpower; so their mornings began with a greenish, milk-free brew of lemongrass and spices, sweetened with local jaggery, and perhaps a bhakri or two to feed the body. Nothing could be more energising than simple wholesome meals. A few weeks later, the men would return to their domestic routines, knowing they had kept the embers of the freedom movement glowing.

One evening, Damodar returned from a rally in Bombay to his rented one-room tenement, energised from the euphoria but actually burning up—he felt sick and nauseous, he nearly fainted—he had contracted jaundice. He spent the next two days alternating between his bed and the single barred window in his room that looked out into the hallway of his chawl, the apartment block with one room tenements of people just like him, students and small families. A neighbour's wife brought him tea and a bhakri once and left him a covered plate of varan bhaat another evening, but for fear of contracting it herself, decided it best to stay away. Her simple varan was nourishing, but she was not prepared to nurse Damodar back to health. She sent word to his friends and a doctor was called. Damodar had been restless, he was often mumbling, sometimes screaming in his sleep. Friends found Damodar in his plain wooden bed, shivering in his cotton pyjamas, unbathed and weak, murmuring over and over again:

"(P'l.. P'l... P'l, Pearl) marry me.."

His young visitors broke out into loud laughter. Damodar was drunk and had mistaken them for women, they thought, and began teasing him. Hearing the rancour, the neighbour's wife stopped in to check. She handed the young men a postcard—it had been delivered earlier that morning— perhaps they should read it to him for it might be from his brother and would cheer him up. The neighbour's wife could not read and the postcard was in English.

As Damodar's friends looked over the postcard, their snickering waned. Damodar's brother was unlikely to write in English. The handwriting was elegant, in deep blue ink, the flimsy piece of paper soiled from the markings of its travel— perhaps it came from far. It bore a single postage stamp in one corner and two postal marks, one each from the Lonavala and Bombay post offices. One friend decided to practice his English and read it out loud:

"My dear Damodar: I hope this postcard finds you in good health. I am doing well. We prepare for David's wedding at the end of the year. I shall be in Pune all of next month with Aunty Beth and Solomon, and will not be able to write to you. I will ask Aunty Beth to send an invitation to your family and will write when I return. Perhaps I will see you at David's wedding. Do stay safe, as always, I shall wait for your next postcard. Regards, Pearl"

There was silence in the room as the young men glanced at each other perplexed; the neighbour's wife who had been peeking through the window and did not understand a word of that postcard wondered if someone died.

Damodar's friends realised that in his jaundice-induced trance, he had been talking to a woman named Pearl. They had no idea that Damodar had been writing to her as he had never once talked about her before.

Damodar's friends nursed him back until he was coherent enough to send word to Pearl—if she turned down his proposal, the jaundice would relapse. She came to see him that week, shaken by his adamant and unusual proposal. Father was away, Aunty Beth would be angry—but she had to visit Damodar. She agreed to be his wife and returned to Lonavala to find a way to convince her family.

The rebellion in Bombay had not subsided. By 1928, Damodar had seen enough. With their college education complete, Damodar and Pearl were going to do something constructive with their lives. One evening in Bombay, in 1929, when Gandhi spoke of unyoking from foreign made items and burning foreign made clothes, Damodar was in the crowds, pledging his commitment to the cause, to wear handmade, locally made clothes—khadi. He traded his tailored pant and coat for a khadi dhoti and a simple kurta with metal buttons, both handspun clothes made by his brethren. He found a cobbler to make him simple sandals and started sporting a Gandhi topi, a flat white side cap reminiscent of the paper boats he made as a child. Pearl had a harder time adjusting to the khadi—she stayed with handspun silks instead just like her father had raised her to wear, a long-sleeved shirt for modesty and a braided bun with flowers in her hair. She had always worn flowers in her hair, it was not unpatriotic to do that, but she needed to embrace 'the freedom movement' for Damodar's sake.

Damodar and Pearl began to plan their life together. The marriage between a Jewish girl and a Brahmin boy would symbolise their act of rebellion, where love conquered and triumphed, where there was hope for the future. But neither family was by their side on this happy occasion, in person or in spirit.

Their young optimism took Damodar and Pearl first to the temple to be married where Pearl converted to the Hindu faith for the sake of her love and became Aruni Damodar Vaidya. With the blessings of the Arya Samaj and the Bombay Municipal Court, they were ready to begin the next phase of their life. It was the early 1930's—they found a small tenement to live in, and set up a small school in the middle of Bombay. Damodar taught elementary English, history, and arithmetic while Aruni did her part by teaching English and French. She had kept up on learning French and it was not a demanding classroom.

Every few months they sent letters and postcards home to their family, telling them of all the wonderful experiences of being a young family. However, neither Damodar nor Aruni found any support. Over the many years that followed, their communications remained one sided as no one wrote back. No one consoled them on the passing of their first-born daughter or congratulated them on the birth of the two boys. Each suggestion of a visit was met with silence and no one came to visit them either. Aruni never quite learned the ways of her Brahmin husband. She missed being among her family, but this was all for love—and what was a greater act of love and sacrifice than giving up one's family? Sumati now had two children of her own and once wrote a postcard to Damodar. She was however caught up with the challenges of domestic life and parenting two of her own and three step-children, while still a young adult herself. Damodar and Aruni wondered if they needed to return to live in Alibag to let their families see their lives in person.

Damodar was following the teachings of Gandhi more closely than before, believing that progress for their country would come through selfless service towards their countrymen. This seemed like a perfect answer—they could mend their relationship with their family while serving the community they grew up in! Damodar and Aruni took these Gandhian values of 'Ahimsa, Trusteeship and Constructive Action' from the national euphoria surrounding them and decided to return to their home and family, to Alibag. Taking their two boys, seven-year-old Tatya and two-year-old Bandu, Damodar and Aruni began a journey to be among people they loved.

It was the summer of 1942 and the schools had been let out. Aruni and Damodar had just sold their school in Bombay and with the money bought a little hut and a tiny piece of land in Pezari, another little coastal hamlet just outside of Alibag. They planned to initially stay in Alibag and convert the hut into a little school, and teach. Perhaps Aruni would finally be able to learn some of the old-fashioned cooking, thought Damodar. He was homesick, quite homesick.

They packed up their belongings and said goodbye to their few friends—boarded the little dingy ferry from the Bhau-cha-dhakka Wharf in Bombay. From here, they would pass through two fishing ports to Dharamtar, a busy little jetty along the bay to the east of Bombay, where they would board a bus that would take them to their childhood homes, to Alibag.

Damodar and Aruni gingerly stepped off the ferry and even though they had done this before, this trip felt different. The boys were brimming with nervous excitement, they had never been to the village, and they had never seen their grandparents!

Bandu exclaimed that the ocean and the salt marshes smelt funny. Tatya reminded him that is where all the fish lived. Perhaps the fishes would find Bandu and Tatya's home funny smelling too. The boys chuckled and laughed. The laughter of the boys calmed their parents' nerves a little—it made them hopeful again.

Aruni did not expect that their hour-long bus ride would feel just as long drawn as the three-hour journey across the bay. Perhaps it was because there were no familiar faces on the bus, or perhaps because no one smiled at her like they used to, or maybe because the conductor barely acknowledged her presence. She wondered what had changed so much about her that they did not recognise her. About six hours after they left their city life for good, they were in Alibag—their childhood home—their native place.

The state transport bus came to a rickety and loud halt at the bus depot. The conductor and the driver nearly jumped out of the moving bus. Everyone was tired, huffing and panting as the sun had grown stronger and harsher—the thunderous monsoons and rain-filled clouds would not come for a few more weeks, it was only May—Aruni overlooked their discomfort. She was excited to bring her children home to where she grew up. Damodar shared her excitement for his own childhood home was not far from hers. Although he had not been invited to Shantaram's wedding, he was eager to meet his sister-in-law—he would call her 'vahini', and vahinis were most often very nice and sisterly to their brother-in-laws—they would take turns spoiling each other. Would she be as fun as Sumati tai? He missed his sister.

They waited as their meagre belongings were unloaded from the rooftop racks of the bus, and took their two bindles and two suitcases to the ticketing booth. Damodar asked if he could leave them there until they could return with Shantaram—he had hoped his brother would have come, perhaps something had urgently kept him away.

The chap at the ticketing booth turned out to be an old classmate. Of course, he said, inviting them to drop by for a cup of tea once they were settled in—now that they both had families, there would be so much to catch up on. Village folks were like that in some way. Pleasantries were exchanged and Damodar felt at ease, the village had not changed so much. He was sure Shantaram would be happy to help him get their things. For now, they just were going home, with only what mattered most—their children.

Damodar and Aruni walked familiar streets filled with makeshift awnings, vegetable sellers, and flower sellers, sitting along dusty paths and small bylanes, all adding to the familiar smells of the village. The sight of clay tiled roofs calmed Damodar's spirits. It was just a little past the lunch hour, and Damodar and the boys were starting to get hungry. There were neatly stacked piles of lemongrass, lemons, ginger on wet gunny bags, baskets of green chillies and cut pumpkins—the guavas looked just ripe to eat, perhaps with a sprinkling of salt and chilli powder would be a nice snack, he would have to come back to grab a few. The vendors were also starting to close down for lunch—Damodar hastily bought a hand of 'elaichi' bananas from the fruit seller so he would not show up empty handed. They would get to experience the taste of 'real' bananas. Tall old coconut palms loomed overhead. Being so close to the sea, the air was humid, just like Bombay, except there was something more to this place. It was home.

One of the flower vendors recognised Damodar and smiled at Aruni, thrust a string-tied bunch of fragrant yellow magnolia flowers in her palms for her braided bun. Aruni had missed this old-fashioned instance and familiarity in the big city. Damodar had missed it all too and unconsciously smiled for he was among his people again.

Meanwhile, Tatya was curious about the little lanes and would run ahead to peer each way as his parents walked behind. Bandu was growing restless in his mother's arms. Aruni could not wait to let the adoring arms of someone else cradle the restless boy or hold his fingers while he stumbled around for a little bit. Their pace quickened.

One last corner before Damodar saw his own home, it was only a short walk away from the bus depot. The little brick house jutted out at an angle, his father had insisted that it be built per the Vastu Shastra principles; the front door faced eastwards to bring in the first rays of the sun. He could see the pale blue walls of the inside of the house from the many barred windows. His grandfather's portrait still hung from the same spot, it had a fresh garland of flowers. But the roof needed repair, the once bright terracotta clay tiles were turning dull grey-green from age. Most of the courtyard had been paved in large tiles, except the space around the tulsi Vrindavan, a rectangular pillar-pot with the holy tulsi plant. A fresh coat of dung plastered the floor around it. But near the stoop, there was freshly drawn rangoli. Someone had lit a lamp there that morning; it looked so peaceful. Damodar was sure that his family would have known they were arriving that day by the 2.30 bus. He half expected to see Sumati tai peek out from the windows to greet them. He could not wait to meet everyone—instead, they were met with silence. Damodar approached his home and called:

"Brother, sister-in-law? Is anyone home? It is me, Damodar, see who has come with me?!"

No one came to the door, so Damodar walked up to the short stoop and rattled the latch. He could hear scuffling and the sound of glass bangles, clink-clink-clink... surely someone was home. A petite woman came to the door; she was dressed in the traditional nav-wari saree. She was a plain looking woman but her brow was furrowed as she raised an angry finger to her lips, shutting the door behind her. Damodar was confused. She was not carrying the customary little welcome plate with a lamp and water, or a bowl of raw rice and water, to welcome the couple home. She was tucking in the end of her sari into her waist, covering her shoulders. She appeared hassled and nearly barked at them:

"Yes, yes, I hear you. I'm not deaf. The household is resting for the afternoon. He (your brother) has an evening pooja to attend to. Come back tomorrow morning, after your breakfast, after ten. Hmm. now I suppose you would want some water."

She retreated into the house once more without leaving room for conversation. Shutting the door behind her and mumbling her annoyance partially under her breath she returned with a small lota of water and a single steel tumbler to share among them. They would have to rest on the stoop. Damodar set down the bananas at the stoop as he pried away Tatya from helplessly trying to climb over to peer through the windows into his grandparent's home. Damodar comforted the children by saying everyone was asleep, they would come back later. Vahini did not ask them to stay for tea or offer them a snack of batatey pohe, or some kothimbir wadi like his Sumati tai would have thrown together in a jiffy. Vahini knew who they were, but offered no signs of welcome or comfort. It was simple, they could not stay.

To cover up their disappointment and protect Damodar's ego, Aruni suggested that they walk over to Aunty Beth's home, her old home. But Aunty Beth was even less welcoming—she proclaimed that Samuel, David, and Solomon were in Pune and she was locking up the house to join them the next day. They were interrupting her afternoon nap. No, they could not stay for tea, there was no room in the house for them and especially little children. They should find another place to spend the evening... it was rather impolite to come unannounced. No, Aunty Beth had not seen a postcard from anyone named Aruni, she said, it was a terrible name anyway. As she shut the door, she muttered to herself, "What a waste of my time." Her eyes had now lowered to the base of the door, her head shaking in discontent as she tried to disguise the guilt of the many lies she had just spoken.

The three brothers were upstairs. Samuel watched from a crack in an upstairs window as his sister and her family walked away. She had abandoned them when she had married a Brahmin man and given up her faith. There was no reason to welcome her now.

Within a few hours of coming to Alibag, Damodar and Aruni's apprehensions of meeting or visiting family had been confirmed. They were not welcome in their own village, and neither were their boys. The young romantics had made more changes than either of their families would accept. The notion that a Hindu boy, and a Brahmin at that, had married beneath himself, relinquished faith, religion and norm, instead had ventured to settle down with a Jewish girl, whose family had no real roots to call their own was bringing needless 'drama' into their little village. They had apparently dishonoured their families. A guest-house would do for the next few days until they could get to their own land, anywhere but here. Perhaps the little hut that existed on their land in Pezari there would become more of a home than the once comfortable and sturdy walls of the homes they grew up in. Their childhood homes had now gone cold and the walls were higher than ever, with no doors to let them in.

Damodar and Aruni lead the boys away from this other house as well. They walked through the same lanes they came through a few minutes ago. The boys were hungry, Damodar purchased a second handful of elaichi bananas for all of them; it was a cheap fix to their hunger pangs. They found a small guest house near the bus stop where they had disembarked not too long ago, passing a confused flower vendor on the way who wondered why they were walking away from their home. Neither Aruni nor Damodar said anything to her, just smiled. The lady at the guest house was unsure—these two were from her own village, what happened to their family? She would make them a quick cup of tea for the afternoon and offered them an early dinner of pithla and bhaat, while the boys could eat some banana-shikran and pol'y, but only if Damodar could bring more bananas.

Aruni watched blankly as her hostess, a stranger, had shown more care towards her family than her own had, offering to shelter them from the heat of the summer, expressing empathy in their plight. The clanking of her hostess's glass bangles seemed comforting, someone cared enough, even if it was in exchange for a small sum of money. Aruni mashed the elaichi bananas slowly and methodically in a small bowl of milk and fed them to her boys. The pithla and pol'y came on a small steel plate, there were a few fixings on the side. As they ate their simple meal, there was only silence.

Even the simple flavours felt good, comforting to Damodar, but Aruni was too hurt to eat—she felt betrayed. Aruni asked her hostess to excuse everyone on account of their exhaustion. She later sat down on a little chair in the living room, staring blankly outside into the hot summer skies, having lost words to approach Damodar—he had a hot temper. Damodar rested on the stoop and later headed over to retrieve their bags from the bus stop. His classmate started to ask, but seeing Damodar's face, decided instead that an enthusiastic reminder his invitation would not be suited to Damodar's mood. Village eyes missed very little, and ears—even less.

The boys were told there was a way to see the ocean—their hostess entrusted them to her daughter and the children walked over to see it. There was little else to do today. The summer sun melted into shadows and everyone was too tired to do more. Damodar had walked back over to his old home but had missed Shantaram by a few minutes. He left without a word—what was left to say?

Back at the guest house, Aruni and the boys slept on cotton mattresses set on the floor while Damodar paced around in the courtyard through the night. The summer nights were cool, refreshing and it was soothing to hear the ocean nearby, but not enough to calm Damodar's anger or soothe his hurt pride.

At daybreak, Damodar announced they were leaving that morning for Pezari. Their hostess was surprised and refused to charge them for their stay. She called them 'gharchech pahune,' or 'family guests.' There were no buses to Pezari, so Damodar and Aruni engaged a horse tonga—they would make their own home on their own terms with their two boys. Perhaps this too was a test, a kind of sacrifice.

Epilogue

Damodar and Aruni embark on a new adventure – looking for acceptance. Do they find it? Does Damodar build his school? How does Pearl adjust? How does the Independence movement impact their lives? What happens to their children? Who do they become?

How does Thakor's life shape up after quitting? What becomes of him? Does he ever return to his village and his mother? What happens to Johari-ba?

What do Ratanlal and Shanta do in Mumbai? Do they prosper? Who does Mani grow up to become?

How do all their lives intersect?

These young men and women have only just begun their journey, some as adults, others as children. Their stories are yet unfinished. Their future holds more. What challenges do they face? What brings them joy or brings them to tears? When do their lives overlap? What kind of conflicts do they face and how do they persevere? How do their kitchens evolve over time?

In the next book, follow in the footsteps of these young men and women, as they become adults, age, and die. Read about the lives they lead and the people and memories they leave behind, in the next book:

NOT FOR YOU: FAMILY NARRATIVES OF DENIAL AND COMFORT FOODS, BOOK TWO
(TURMERIC PRESS, FALL, 2017)

...NOT FOR YOU...
RECIPES
...BOOK ONE...

Recipes notes.

These are traditional old-fashioned family recipes that use many unprocessed ingredients. Where convenient alternatives are available, those are listed.

To adjust to spice levels, or make diet-based substitutions without changing the taste, please refer to 'Crack the Code: Cook Any Indian Meal with Confidence' (2016).

Preparation times and cooking times are based on an average working cooking equipment, and results will vary based on the efficiency and performance of individual kitchen equipment and skill level. Please allow additional time the first time you make a recipe to allow for a comfortable cooking pace.

Storage times are approximate and the freshness depends on a variety of factors including freshness of the raw materials and storage conditions. Please use these as suggested times and not absolute.

These recipes use a house blend of spices and masalas such as Goda masala and garam masala. Store bought masalas and spices may be used, however each brand has its own flavor combination. Experimenting with different brands is advisable.

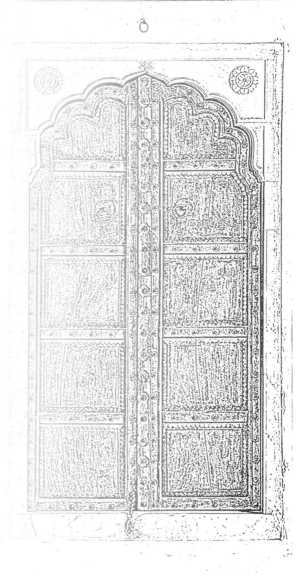

• Bajra Rotlo: Griddle-baked Pearl Millet Bread

Makes: 3-4 8" rotlas or breads
Cook Time: 30 minutes

Ingredients
½ cup water
Pinch of salt
¼ tbsp ghee
1 cup pearl millet flour plus extra for dredging

Method
Set ½ cup water to boil with a pinch of salt & ¼ tbsp ghee. When it boils, remove from heat, mix in the flour. Using a spoon with a heavy handle, stir vigorously, cover and set aside.
When cool enough to handle but still warm, knead the mix and divide into golf ball sized pieces of dough. Dredge with pearl millet flour and roll out into ¼" thick rotlo. On a hot crepe pan or a griddle, get ready to cook each bhakri. Sprinkle water on one side of the uncooked rotlo and place wet side down onto the hot pan. Keep the heat to medium-low. Allow the rotlo to cook undisturbed for a minute until it develops light spots. Move it around the pan to ensure it does not stick. Cook for another minute on medium low. Sprinkle water on the upper side of the rotlo and flip it over. Using a paper towel wad, gently press down on the rotlo to ensure it cooks through. Flip over and repeat on the other side. If it still appears undercooked, cook directly over the open flame for twenty seconds on each side, rotating often to cook evenly. When both sides are cooked, remove from the heat and apply a light layer of ghee on one side. Keep covered with a kitchen towel until ready to eat.

• Chaas: Spiced Buttermilk

Makes: 10, 8 oz servings
Cook Time: 10 minutes

Ingredients
1 tsp toasted cumin seeds, crushed
2 cups unflavored Greek yoghurt
2-3 cups water
Salt, to taste

Method
Pour the yoghurt into a large, deep stockpot or a water jug. Whisk the yoghurt until smooth in consistency. Slowly add a cup of water at a Cook Time and blend in. After all the water is added, the yogurt-water mixture should be similar in consistency to 2% milk. Add additional water if necessary. Add salt. When ready to serve, blend in the toasted and crushed cumin seeds, whisk thoroughly before each pour. Serve at room temperature.

• Jowar Rotlo: Griddle-baked Sorghum Bread

Use the same recipe as for Bajra Rotlo, except change out the Bajra flour for Jowar flour.

Lasan-ni-Chutney: Spicy Garlic Chutney

Makes: 2 cups chutney
Cook Time: 30-40 minutes

Ingredients
4 tbsp oil
1 tsp cumin seeds
1 tsp white sesame seeds
10-12 whole dried red chillies
1½ cups peeled garlic cloves
¼ cup raw unsalted peanuts
2 tbsp lemon juice
1 tsp salt

Method
Lightly dry-roast the peanuts. When cool enough to handle, husk the peanuts and set aside.

Heat the oil in a large saucepan. When the oil is warm but not smoking, add cumin seeds and sesame seeds, and reduce the heat; if the oil is too hot, the sesame seeds will burn. Stir constantly until the seeds are just lightly fried. Stir in the dried red chillies and garlic cloves. Raise the heat to medium-high and cook for 2-3 minutes, stirring constantly. Add the husked peanuts and cook until the peanuts appear lightly toasted. Reduce the heat and add lemon juice and salt and stir well so the flavors are well distributed. Remove from heat when the peanuts are just turning golden. Allow to cool completely and then grind in a food processor to a coarse consistency. Store in a dry container in the refrigerator for 4-6 weeks.

Johari-Ba's Laapsi: Sweet Cracked Wheat Pilaf

Makes: 6-8 servings
Cook Time: 30-45 minutes

Ingredients
2-4 tbsp ghee
3-4 green cardamom pods (optional)
2 cups cracked whole wheat, see pre-prep note
1½ cups water, boiling hot
⅓ cup sugar, adjust to taste
¼ cup almonds, slivered or sliced (optional)
¼ cup or more home-made ghee, to finish (optional)

Method
Rinse the cracked wheat in cold water, drain and set aside.

Heat the ghee in a medium, heavy-bottom saucepan. Turn down the heat to medium-low and add the whole cardamom pods, if using, allow them to release their flavours on medium-low heat for 1-2 minutes. Add the rinsed cracked wheat. Using a flat spatula, stir continuously for 3-5 minutes until the cracked wheat is glistening and coated with the ghee. Reduce the heat to low and carefully add the boiling water. Allow the water to boil through and let the cracked wheat to cook completely. If it still appears undercooked, add ½ cup more water and let it finish cooking, until all the water is absorbed. Finally, add the sugar and almonds, if using any. Cook until the sugar fully dissolves. Adjust for sweetness with additional sugar. Drizzle melted ghee over the finished laapsi just before serving; this dish may be served cold or warm.

• Ek-Anna Kanda Bhajiya: One 'Penny' Batter-fried Onion Rings

Makes: Varies
Cook Time: 30 minutes

INGREDIENTS
2 large red or white onions, cut into ¼" thick rings, separated
BATTER
1 tbsp cumin seeds
½ tsp turmeric powder
2 tbsp cayenne pepper powder
2 cups besan (chickpea flour), sifted
1 tsp baking soda
Salt, to taste
1 to 1½ cups water
Oil for frying

METHOD
In a large bowl, combine all the dry batter Ingredients well until there are no lumps. Make a well in the centre and whisk in one cup of water to make a thick and smooth batter. Break up any lumps that form. Once the batter is smooth, add in about ½ cup of water or enough until it reaches a pancake batter consistency. Set this aside for 10 minutes until ready to use.
Heat the oil in a fryer until it reaches 400°F. Leave the fryer basket submerged in the oil. Work with small batches of onions rings. Toss each small batch into the batter until each piece is well coated. Using a large fork, scoop out the batter-coated onion rings and quickly but carefully drop them into the hot oil. Move them around gently to ensure each ring has room to fry. The onion rings will cook within 2-3 minutes to a golden brown. Remove them all at once and drain on a tray lined with paper towels. Continue to fry all the remaining onion rings in a similar manner. Transfer each batch to a serving tray after they have drained. Serve hot immediately.

• Green Mango & Coconut Chutney

Makes: 2 cups chutney
Cook Time: 30 minutes

INGREDIENTS
1 tsp cumin seeds
1" fresh ginger
2 or more jalapeños, seeded (optional)
1 cup fresh or frozen coconut meat, unsweetened
½ small raw mango, diced into small pieces
2 cups fresh cilantro leaves and stems, washed
¼ tsp sugar
Splash of lemon juice
Salt, to taste

METHOD
In a medium food processor bowl, combine the cumin seeds, ginger, jalapeño, coconut, diced mango, cilantro, lemon juice, sugar, salt and ¼ cup water. Blend on medium-low into coarse but even mixture. Thin out with water as needed. Check for salt and heat, adjust as needed. Store in a clean, dry glass jar for up to 2 days in the refrigerator.

Sukka Mutton: Charcoal-Grilled Meat Kebabs

Makes: 8 servings
Cook Time: 30-40 minutes

Ingredients
2 lbs. goat or lamb meat, boneless, skinless, cut into bite-sized pieces
1 cup boiler onions, skin on
Marinade
2 tbsp ginger paste
½ cup unflavored 2% unflavoured Greek yoghurt, whisked
2 tsp cayenne pepper powder, adjust to taste
1 tsp salt
2 tbsp lemon juice
8-10 metal or wooden/bamboo skewers, see pre-prep note.

Pre-Prep
Oil the metal skewers prior to use. If using wooden/bamboo skewers, presoak for at least two hours to prevent them from burning.

Method
Trim the top and bottom of the boiler onions, leave the skin on.
Combine the marinade ingredients in a large glass bowl. Trim and cut the meat into 2" pieces. Add the meat into the marinade, season with salt, coat evenly and chill for at least 20 minutes.
Arrange the marinated meat pieces on skewers. On a separate skewer, thread the onions though their centre. Cook the meat skewers on a charcoal grill (approx. 450°F, ten minutes until tender). Rotate the skewer regularly to prevent from burning. In the last 3-4 minutes cook the skewer of the onions on the charcoal grill as well, letting the onion skins burn away as they cook. Serve hot.

• Kolhapuri Matki Misal: Turkish Gram or Moth Beans in A Coconut Stew

Makes: 8 servings
Cook Time: 30-40 minutes

Ingredients
2 tbsp oil
1 cup diced yellow or white onions
1 tsp ginger paste
1 tsp garlic paste
1 fresh jalapeño, finely chopped (optional)
¼ tsp Goda masala, optional (you can use powdered garam masala instead)
¼ tsp turmeric powder
1½ tsp Kolhapuri cayenne pepper powder (or regular cayenne pepper powder)
¾ tsp cumin powder
¾ tsp coriander powder
¼ cup grated mature coconut flesh
1 cup dried matki beans (Turkish Gram or Moth beans), see pre-prep note
¼ cup water, or as needed
1 tsp salt
1 cup fresh diced tomatoes
½ tsp sugar
Garnish (optional)
2 tbsp oil
2 tsp black mustard seeds
1/8 tsp hing (asafetida powder)
2-3 fresh curry leaves (optional)

Pre-Prep
Soak the matki beans in about 2 cups of water overnight. Discard the water the next morning, and boil in a large saucepan with 3-4 cups of water until tender. Set aside. Alternately, cook the beans in 2 cups of water in a pressure cooker for 10 minutes. Allow this to cool completely before using.

Method
Heat the oil in a large saucepan. Add the onions and sauté until lightly golden brown. Then add the ginger and garlic paste and jalapeños, if using any, and sauté until fragrant. Add the goda masala and sauté for 10-20 seconds. Carefully add the turmeric, cayenne pepper powder, cumin powder and coriander powder, give it a quick stir and add the freshly grated coconut, sautéing for 1-2 minutes until it loses some of its liquid. Remove from the heat.
Once this mixture has cooled down, grind into a smooth sauce. Return to the saucepan and resume cooking. Add the pre-cooked matki beans, gently mix until they are evenly covered by the sauce. Cover the pot lightly to allow the steam to escape. Cook for about 8-10 minutes. Stir every few minutes to cook evenly and to ensure that the beans do not stick to the bottom of the pot. Season with salt, sugar and tomatoes, cover and cook for another 3-5 minutes until the tomatoes soften.
For the garnish: In a separate small saucepan, heat the oil. When hot but not smoking, add the mustard seeds and let them pop. Turn off the heat and add asafetida and curry leaves if using, and let it sizzle. Pour this mixture over the finished cooked matki beans. Serve hot with bhakri or steamed rice.

Kolmbi: Spicy Shrimp in Tomatoes

Makes: 8 servings
Cook Time: 30 minutes

Ingredients
2 tbsp oil
½ cup diced yellow or white onions
1 tsp ginger paste
1 tsp garlic paste
¼ tsp turmeric powder
1½ tsp cayenne pepper powder
¾ tsp cumin powder
¾ tsp coriander powder
½ cup diced tomatoes
¼ cup water
1-1½ lb shelled and deveined uncooked shrimp or prawns
½ tsp salt (or to taste)
¼ cup cilantro leaves for garnish (optional)

Method
Heat the oil in a large saucepan. Add the onions and sauté until lightly golden. Then add the ginger and garlic paste and sauté until fragrant. Add the turmeric, cayenne pepper powder, cumin powder and coriander powder. Add the diced tomatoes and water, and let this mixture cook on medium-low for a few minutes until it becomes a thick sauce. Add the shrimp or prawns, mix well and lightly cover to cook for about 5-7 minutes until the shrimp is cooked. Season with salt and garnish with cilantro leaves. Serve hot with warm bread of choice.

Mur'mur'ya c'a Chiwda: Quick Puffed Rice Mix

Makes: Varies
Cook Time: 20 minutes

Ingredients
¼ cup oil
1 tsp cumin seeds
3" fresh ginger, grated
12-15 fresh curry leaves
3-4 whole dried red chillies, broken into ¼" pieces
¼ tsp hing (asafetida powder)
¼ cup raisins
½ cup raw unsalted peanuts
¼ cup store bought sev (spicy lentil noodles)
¼ cup unsweetened dried coconut slices (optional)
6 cups unsweetened rice puffs (such as Rice Krispies®)
1 tsp salt
2 tbsp sugar
2 tbsp lime juice

Method
Sift and pick through the puffed rice, discard discoloured pieces. Dry roast the puffed rice until it is toasty but not coloured. Spread over a paper towel to allow moisture to wick away. Let it cool.
Heat the oil in a large wok. Add cumin seeds, ginger, curry leaves and chopped jalapeños. Stir vigorously to season the oil well, reduce the heat. Add dried red chillies, asafetida powder and turmeric powder; stir vigorously to avoid burning. Add the raisins and peanuts, allow them to cook. As the peanuts begin to roast, add the salt, sugar and lime juice; turn off the heat. While the oil and spices are still hot, add the cooled toasted puffed rice and sev in small batches. Toss with two flat spatulas with each addition until all the rice is mixed in. Return the wok to a medium-low heat and toss this mixture quickly. Remove from heat. Serve hot or allow to cool and store it in an airtight container for up to four weeks.

PINEAPPLE MALPUA (FRITTERS)

Makes: 8 servings
Cook Time: 20-30 minutes

INGREDIENTS
½ cup milk
1 egg
2 cardamom pods, crushed fine
¼ cup sugar
⅔ cup all-purpose flour
⅓ cup fine semolina
2 tbsp. freshly grated coconut, optional
¼ tsp salt
1 tsp vanilla, optional
8-10 thick cut pineapple slices
Cooking oil for deep frying

To serve
½ cup heavy whipping cream
2-3 tbsp. sugar
8-10 saffron strands
1-2 tbsp. sugar, optional

PRE-PREP
Whisk the heavy whipping cream with sugar and saffron to stiff peaks. Cover and set aside in the refrigerator until ready to use.
If using canned pineapple, drain the slices, set them on a paper towel or in a colander to drain for 15-20 minutes before use. If using fresh pineapple, pat them dry and set aside until ready to use.
Whisk the milk, egg, cardamom powder and sugar together in a shallow bowl until the sugar has completely dissolved. Stir in the all-purpose flour, semolina, salt, fresh coconut and vanilla (if using) to make a thick smooth batter, ensuring there are no lumps. Cover and set aside for 45 minutes. Check to see if all the semolina is moist and softened before using it to make the fritters.

METHOD
Heat cooking oil in a suitable frying pan (oil must be at least 3 inches deep to allow the fritters to fry well). Test the oil with a drop of batter--if the batter rises to the top immediately, the oil is hot enough. Reduce the heat to medium low.

Carefully dip single pineapple slices into the batter and turn each slice once to coat fully; do not turn over more than once as the slice can break. Hold each batter covered slice over the batter pan to let extra batter drip away. Carefully lower the pineapple slice, one at a time, into the hot oil. Do not crowd the oil with too many pineapple slices, as they cook quickly and need the room when you turn them over. Fry until each side is lightly golden brown, about one minute on each side. If the batter is browning quickly, reduce the heat to low. Once each side is cooked, using a spider or strainer carefully remove each fritter and set aside to drain on a paper towel for 2-3 minutes to cool. Do the same with all remaining pineapple slices.

Serve the pineapple malpua's at room temperature with a side of the saffron whipped cream. Dust with granulated sugar for extra sparkle.

Varan: Plain Yellow Daal

Makes: 8 servings
Cook Time: 20-30 minutes

Ingredients
1 tbsp ghee or butter
1 tsp cumin seeds
10 fresh curry leaves
1 fresh jalapeño, split lengthwise
¼ tsp turmeric powder
2 cups precooked toor daal (skinless split pigeon peas)
½ cup water
Salt to taste

Garnish:
Splash of lemon juice
Chopped cilantro, optional
To serve: Steamed rice

Method
Heat the ghee in a small heavy-bottom saucepan. As it heats up, add the cumin seeds, curry leaves and fresh jalapeños (if using) allow them to sizzle. Turn the heat down to low, add the turmeric powder and stir in to let it cook slightly. Do not let it burn. Immediately add the pre-cooked toor daal and a half cup of water to and stir. Cook for 2-3 minutes, stir regularly to prevent the daal from settling or sticking to the bottom of the saucepan. Season with salt; add a splash of lemon juice and garnish with chopped cilantro. Serve hot over steamed rice.

SATYAGRAHI CHA: A FREEDOM FIGHTER'S TEA

Makes: 4 servings
Cook Time: 10 minutes

INGREDIENTS
2 cups water
1 entire leaflet of lemongrass or about 8-10, 2" pieces
1 tbsp whole coriander seeds
¼ tsp dried ginger powder
1" jaggery piece

METHOD
Set the water to boil in a saucepan. When the water begins a gentle boil, add the lemongrass leaflets to the water and let this simmer for 3 minutes on medium-low. The water will pick up a pale green hue, this is normal. Add the whole coriander seeds and dried ginger powder and allow this to simmer for another minute. Simmer longer if you want a stronger decoction. Strain into desired container. Serve with a side of jaggery.
Jaggery may be dissolved into the tea itself if desired or may be consumed alongside the tea itself.

EL-CHI KELYA-CHE SHIKRAN: FINGER OR BABY BANANA'S IN MILK

Makes: 2 servings
Assembly Time: 5-10 minutes

INGREDIENTS
1 cup room temperature or warm milk
3-4 finger bananas or baby bananas, diced
2 tsp or more sugar, to taste
½ tsp or more cardamom powder (optional)

METHOD
In a serving bowl, mash half the bananas in the milk. Add the sugar and cardamom powder to flavour the milk to taste. Add the remaining bananas just before serving. Serve as is or with pol'ya or bhakri.

• Ghadi-chya Pol'ya: Layered Whole Wheat Griddle-fried Bread

Makes: 12-15 8" pol'ya
Cook Time: 30-45 minutes

Ingredients
3 cups atta (stone-ground durum whole wheat flour), sifted, plus extra for dredging
⅔ cup or more water for binding
Salt, to taste
½ tsp oil
2 tbsp ghee

Special Tools: Tapered rolling pin; flat, raised and stable rolling platform

Method
Using a food processor fitted with an S-blade or in a large bowl, combine the flour with salt and enough water to make a firm dough. The dough should be firm but not hard, moist but not wet, and similar in consistency to Play-Doh®. Carefully knead the oil into the dough and cover with a clear wrap until ready to roll.

To Roll: Divide the dough into golf ball-sized pieces. Using the palms of your hands, roll each piece into a smooth ball and lightly flatten to make 1" diskettes. Keep these covered to avoid drying. Dredge only the diskette you are going to roll in the dry flour. Using a tapered rolling pin, gently roll out the dough using the pressure of your hands to make it move slightly and spin/rotate. Moving the rolling pin along a small circular path, rolling outwards but not over the edge, roll until it is a four-inch disk. Apply a small amount of melted ghee all over one side of the disk and fold the disk over itself, first into a half. Apply some ghee to the exposed half, and fold it over itself again into another half, to yield a pie-shaped piece of folded dough. Dredge/dust this with dry flour to avoid stickiness. Very lightly repeat rolling out the dough, although this Cook Time the dough is less likely to spin. Continue rolling it out until the dough is uniformly about 1/8th" thick. Lightly dust off the uncooked pol'y.
To Cook: Heat a shallow nonstick pan on medium-high heat. When ready to place the pol'y in the pan, turn it down to medium heat. The side that hits the pan first is the first side. Watch the dough bubble slightly and move it around in the pan without flipping it over. Turn it over approximately one minute later. The first side should be lightly spotted but not have dark spots. If spots appear too quickly, reduce the heat. Repeat on the second side, and while the second side cooks, lightly baste the first side with ghee. Using a spatula, flip the pol'y and repeat the basting. Both sides should have ghee-cooked once without ghee and once with ghee. Remove from heat and cover with a paper towel or a colander to help the steam evaporate. Once they have come to room temperature, the pol'ys can be transferred to an appropriate storage container.

PITHLA': CHICKPEA GRAVY

Makes: 4-6 servings
Cook Time: 20 minutes

INGREDIENTS
1 tsp oil
1 tsp cumin seeds
1 tsp black mustard seeds
¼ cup white onions, finely chopped
1 tsp fresh garlic paste (optional)
5-6 fresh curry leaves
1-2 jalapeños split lengthwise
¼ tsp hing (asafetida powder)
¼ tsp turmeric powder
1 cup chickpea flour, sifted
½ cup water, add extra as needed
½ cup unflavored 2% Greek yoghurt
Salt, to taste

GARNISH:
Cilantro leaves from 4-5 stems, finely chopped (optional)
To serve: Steamed rice

METHOD
Whisk the chickpea flour with water, yoghurt, salt and chopped coriander leaves, set aside until ready to use.
Heat the oil in a small heavy-bottom saucepan. As it heats up, add the mustard seeds, cumin seeds and allow them to season the oil as the mustard seeds crack open. Add the onions, garlic paste, curry leaves and jalapeños (if using), cook to soften. Turn the heat down to low, add the turmeric powder and hing, and stir in to let it cook slightly. Do not let it burn. Immediately add the prepared chickpea sauce and stir vigorously. Continue stirring for 3-4 minutes until the gravy thickens and begins to leave the side of the pan. Add water to change the consistency of the gravy as desired. Garnish with chopped cilantro (if using). Serve hot over steamed rice or with pol'y.

Select Reading

Bandyopadhyaya, Sekhara: From Plassey to Partition: A History of Modern India, 2004

Chandavarkar, Rajnarayan: The Origins of Industrial Capitalism in India: Business Strategies and the Working Classes in Bombay, 1900-1940 (Cambridge South Asian Studies), 2003

Dwivedi, Sharada, Mehrotra Rahul: Bombay: The cities within, India Book House, 1995

Manwaring, Alfred: Marathi Proverbs, Clarendon Press, 1899

Molesworth, James Thomas, Padmanji, Baba: A Compendium of Molesworth's Marathi and English Dictionary, Bombay Education Society, 1863

Rajputana (Agency): The Rajputana Gazetteer, By, Volume III, Simla, Central Government Press, 1880

Riddick, John F. : The History of British India: A Chronology, Greenwood Publishing Group, 2006

Rohatgi, Pauline (Editor), Godrej, Pheroza (Editor): Bombay to Mumbai: Changing Perspectives, Marg Foundation, 1997

Sarup & Sons, Rajasthan Through the Ages - Rajasthan (India), 2008

Other Books By Author

A Dozen Ways to Celebrate: Twelve Decadent Feasts For the Culinary Indulgent, Turmeric Press, 2014, Ebook ISBN: 978-1-940957-00-5, Paperback ISBN: 978-1-940957-12-8

Five Vegetarian, Gluten-Free Feasts, Turmeric Press, 2014, Ebook ISBN: 978-1-940957-02-9

The Family Feast, Turmeric Press, 2014, Ebook ISBN: 978-1-940957-07-4

Crack The Code: Cook Any Indian Meal With Confidence, Foreword by Faye Levy, Second Edition, Turmeric Press, 2016, Ebook ISBN: 978-1-940957-06-7, Paperback ISBN: 978-1-940957-08-1

Roti: Easy Indian Breads & Sides, Turmeric Press, 2016, Ebook ISBN: 978-1-940957-11-1

Not For You: Family Narratives of Denial & Comfort Foods: Book One, Turmeric Press, 2017, Ebook ISBN: 978-1-940957-13-5, Paperback ISBN: 978-1-940957-14-2

Upcoming Titles

Not For You: Family Narratives of Denial & Comfort Foods: Book Two, Turmeric Press, 2017

Roti: Easy Indian Breads & Sides, Second Edition, Turmeric Press, 2017

Contact

Nandita Godbole
currycravings@gmail.com
www.currycravings.com
Twitter/IG: @currycravings